JUST CALL ME LUCKY

[handwritten inscription: To May messing with Luck for a Friend for ever. "Lucky" Eddie Rack]

THE EDDIE RACK STORY

BY EDDIE RACK
WITH GENO LAWRENZI

DEDICATION

Dedicated to my wife, Genevieve, with thanks for those wonderful, loving years.

Genevieve and Eddie Rack pose in the Rack's front yard in Boston, PA in the early 1940s. In the background, away from the view of the camera, is the 9-hole golf course Eddie and his two brothers built. "We used Campbell's Soup cans for holes," Rack recalled.

TABLE OF CONTENTS

FOREWORD
By Arnold Palmer

I've had occasion over the years to author forewords and prefaces for quite a few books documenting the histories of some of our most prestigious golf and country clubs, private and often exclusive establishments that have played important roles in the annals of golf in America. In some ways this book falls in the same category, yet at the same time it is in clear contrast. It relates a heartwarming rags-to-riches life story of the son of immigrant parents, his extended family and his friends whose contributions to the game have been primarily in the public course realm.

My acquaintanceship with Eddie Rack goes back a long way. As this narrative tells us, Eddie was a fine amateur in Western Pennsylvania. He played the country club circuit as a member of Youghiogheny, where he was first exposed to the game as a six-year-old, long before he made his real mark on Western Pennsylvania golf with the 7 Springs golf course and his long service as a member of the Tri-State section of the Professional Golfers Association of America. I remember the day in 1955 when I went to Youghiogheny to play in a charity exhibition. I had turned pro the year before and was making my first run on the national PGA Tour. Many of the best players in Western Pennsylvania, pros and amateurs, played in the Youghiogheny event. I shot 71, but my playing partner, Eddie Rack, then the Youghiogheny club champion, beat me by two shots.

Having grown up at Latrobe Country Club, having been around golf courses and clubs all of my life and owning two clubs myself right now, I know what Eddie and his family have gone through in making 7 Springs so sucessful as one of the finest public courses in Western Pennsylvania and more recently in turning around the floundering Colony West club in Tamarac, Florida. Running a golf course can be a very difficult, all-consuming task. The Rack family merit the recognition that this book brings to what they have achieved, especially considering that the patriarch wiped out a medical death sentence years ago when he made a miraculous — he calls it lucky — recovery from inoperable liver cancer.

Eddie Rack tells the main story in this book, but his literary collaborator, Geno Lawrenzi, wisely interviewed and intertwined the narrative with observations from just about every living family member, associate and close friends of this always genial man to give it greater perspective. This book is an easy and interesting read.

Arnold Palmer

INTRODUCTION

By Geno Lawrenzi Jr.

Books are wonderful creatures. You never know when one is going to pop in on you and say, "Write me. This is good!"

Credit this one, "Just Call Me Lucky: The Eddie Rack Story," to my younger brother, John, known to the world of gospel music lovers as Legs Lawrenzi. Yeah, brother, I owe you one.

My brother, and his gospel group, the Steel City Quartet, had been booked to sing at Eddie Rack's 90th birthday celebration. On the day of the bash, he mentioned it to me. Both of us had caddied at the Youghiogheny Country Club for Eddie and his friends during the 1950s.

"It's going to be quite an event," said my brother. "Why don't you come along? I'm sure Eddie Rack wouldn't mind. After all, you were a Yough caddy in those days and there aren't many of us left."

I was sure that Eddie, being the gentleman he is, wouldn't mind my crashing his birthday party. But I had a date that night and begged off the second-hand invitation. "Just tell me what happens," I said, and we left it at that.

The next day, Legs filled me with the details of the evening. How Eddie's golf friends from all over the Monongahela Valley had been there, how he had given an emotional speech about growing up the son of a poor coal miner, how he and his family had managed to acquire two valuable golf courses and how it had all come to pass because of a series of circumstances most of us would call luck.

"You should have been there, Brother," Legs said. "It was very moving."

His words began to eat on me. I thought of how my brothers and I had grown up in a coal mining family, and how my father had worked in the mines until opportunity came his way and he quit his job to join U.S. Steel Corporation's Irvin Works in nearby Dravosburg. The similarity in our lives was unquestionable. Eddie and I had both been caddies, we had grown up poor. Our fathers had been coal miners. Eddie had gone on to wealth and success, while I had become a journalist, book writer and magazine writer.

With those thoughts in mind, I decided to approach him about writing a book.

One thing you have got to understand about Eddie Rack: he makes no important decision without discussing it with his family.

He liked the idea of a book, and it wasn't because of ego or the thought of making money. Eddie simply wanted to tell the story of how the Rack family had pulled together to make a success of life. That's all. Just the story of a man from poor beginnings who defied the odds to end up the owner of two major golf courses in Pennsylvania and Florida.

Faxes and e-mails flew between Pennsylvania

and Florida. In less than a week, the family had decided to go with the book. First things first, though. Eddie was having problems with a cataract in his right eye and needed surgery to relieve the pressure. No problem. The 90-year-old went in, had the operation and came out, ready to be interviewed for his autobiography.

One of the first things we talked about was an event that happened on a special day in August 1951. I was 13 and had just graduated from grade school. Eddie was scheduled to play a match against Arnold Palmer at the Youghiogheny Country Club and my brothers and I were there to watch.

"How could I forget that day?," said Rack. "I shot a 69, Arnie shot a 71 and I beat him."

"I know. I followed you and Palmer around the golf course," I said. "It was one of the biggest days of my life, watching the two of you play."

Rack just shook his head in disbelief. Talk about coincidence! I don't know if it helped, but when we approached Arnold Palmer about writing a forward to the book and told him about that day in August, he didn't hesitate. He would be proud to make his small contribution to the book, he said, citing his ties to the area and the fact his father had been a friend of Rack's. There are few people around classier than Arnold Palmer. He is a man who remembers his roots.

As I write this, it is late July. The mid-day temperature is hovering around 90 and the humidity is high. The weather forecaster predicts rain.

From my second story apartment window at Rego's Hotel in downtown Charleroi, I can see people scurrying back and forth on cars and on foot. I find myself thinking of my days as a caddy. It didn't pay much, but I loved the work. My brothers and I would hitchhike to the golf course (Sometimes we would walk the entire five miles when nobody stopped to pick us up). Our objective was to arrive there as early as possible so we would be first on the caddy master's list and get out early. After the first 18-hole round, which would take anywhere from three to five hours, depending on the speed of the foursome, we would wait around for another job. Sometimes I would caddy for three golfers in a day, working until it was nearly impossible to see the ball in the darkness. After collecting money, I would head down the road, walking past Mt. Vernon Cemetery, with my thumb stretched out for motorists to see. I learned how it felt to be independent, to be free, and to be able to earn money to help my family. That's pretty much the way Eddie started out, as you will see from this book.

When you think about it, Eddie Rack did not accomplish anything extraordinary in making his way to the top. All he did was the things we were all taught to do by our parents: be honest, work hard, keep your word, treat your family and friends as you would like to be treated, and apply the work ethic to everything you do. The rest will take care of itself. It's basic and it's simple. And yet how many of us really do this and do it right? Eddie Rack did it right and the rewards, as you will soon see, were far beyond anything he could ever have expected.

Every book should be dedicated to somebody. This is my third book to be published. The others,

"Lord, Why Me?" and "How To Win At Blackjack," failed to make much of an impact on the literary world, even though they had their share of readers. Being a person who has made his living by writing, I have long been gratified by the way the public has accepted my fictional short stories, articles, poetry and even a couple of screenplays I had the privilege to work on. To my way of thinking, because of the subject content and the way it came about, this is the first "real" book I have written. For that opportunity and pleasure, I owe much to my brother, Legs, and to the Eddie Rack family.

Eddie Rack has dedicated this book to his lovely wife, Genevieve. She is a great woman, a classy lady who deserves the dedication.

I would like to remember my late parents, Dorothy and Geno Lawrenzi. Anyone who has ever visited our home on top of Sutersville Hill will have something to say about the hospitality of the Lawrenzi family. It always included good food, conversation, friendship and a glass of homemade wine.

I also want to pay special tribute to my former wife, Nan Isbell, of Cullman, AL, who stayed at my side for 19 years and produced two incredible children. She always encouraged my writing and waited patiently for that book I had always promised her. I would also like to acknowledge my son, James Dale, who will become the Lawrenzi family's first heart surgeon, and my daughter, Rossana Lawrenzi, who is attending college in Springfield, MO and who is planning a new career launch.

Ghostwriting a book isn't easy. It has its own unique responsibilities and challenges. Compare it to the problems that go with making a marriage work, and you'll get some idea of the pitfalls that accompany any book writing project. I feel very lucky that Eddie Rack is the subject of this book. He's a good person to interview. He was a book waiting to happen.

We worked in a variety of settings, usually at our own private table at 7 Springs. On a couple of occasions, we met at his home along the golf course. And I spent a memorable week visiting his son, Norm, and the entourage at Colony West in Tamarac, FL. Eddie and his family members always answered all my questions, never holding anything back. To the extended Rack family as well as the family friends who contributed to this book, I say, thanks. All of you were terrific. If this book is a success, give them the credit.

Let me know what you think of this book. Perhaps you have a book of your own to write, or know of someone who has a story to tell. I'll listen. It may not have the impact of "Just Call Me Lucky: The Eddie Rack Story," but I promise to listen. And, who knows: maybe we can make your dream into a reality. My e-mail address is lawrenzi@hotmail.com.

Now sit back, relax and read, *Just Call Me Lucky: The Eddie Rack Story*.

"ANALYZING THE GAME OF GOLF"

We were seated around a table in Eddie and Genevieve Rack's living room. Their spacious home lies in a lovely wooded area along the scenic 7 Springs Golf Course next to Route 48 just outside Elizabeth, PA. The country is made up of rolling hills, with verdant greenery and tall shade trees. From their large picture window, you can see giant oaks and sycamores. The place gives you a feeling of splendid isolation.

"Would you gentlemen like more donuts and coffee?" his wife asks. Eddie says no, and I thank her as she refills my cup. We begin.

Q: Aside from the fact that golf has made you wealthy, what is it about the game that you like best? Bobby Jones, the legendary golfer who made his mark in the 1920s and 1930s by winning the British Amateur, British Open, United States Open, the

U.S. Amateur and many other competitions, including the Grand Slam, wrote in his best-selling autobiography, "Golf Is My Game," the following: "Golfers know and have known for a long time that when playing golf, it is almost impossible to think of anything else." He noted that is why so many business owners, celebrities and even Presidents play the game so much. Could you please comment on this statement?

A: Well, it certainly opens the field for you to meet people. When I started playing, only the rich and influential played golf. You'd never see a poor man with a golf club in his hands. With golf, you have to be focused and stay focused. I just enjoyed playing the game. I never thought it would make a name for me. Golf was enjoying the end results, a desire for perfection. Every shot a golfer hits is a creative shot, designed specifically for that situation. They're all different.

Q: Some of the most successful golfers of all time came up as caddies, just as you did. People like Arnold Palmer, Gene Sarazen, Ben Hogan and Byron Nelson, to name just a few. They learned to play golf like my brothers and I learned to play baseball, on sandlots and in cow pastures, just playing, playing and playing because they liked the game. How does this fit in with the way you feel about the game?

A: I started caddying at the Youghiogheny Country Club at the age of six. I certainly never thought I would turn into a golfer. All I was doing was giving a service to well-to-do people who would pay me for my labor. Well, the service paid off in ways I could never have dreamed. They put me under their wings and literally drug me along to success. They influenced my decisions and me and helped bring me to the top. When I was on the course caddying, I had the opportunity to watch golfers, good and bad, hit the ball. It didn't take a rocket scientist to realize that by imitating the good players, you would play better. When I was caddying, I always knew before the round ended if the golfer would shoot a 75 or a 95. You could tell from his swing, temperament and even the clubs he had in his bag. If they were run of the mill clubs, he would probably be a run of the mill golfer. The established golfers always had the better clubs.

Q: You and Bobby Jones had a lot in common. Like you, Bobby was only six when he started playing. His father, who was an attorney and who had a passion for golf, gave him an old iron he had no use for, a cleek.

A: (Eddie laughs). Yeah, I know what a cleek was. A two-iron.

A: Exactly. An iron club with a half-inch wide blade and a loft that approximated a two-iron. Bobby started going around the golf course with just that cleek, hitting the ball and even using it as a putter.

Q: What was your first golf club?

A: My family and I lived on a 14-acre farm in Pigeon Hollow just outside Boston, PA. My brothers and I made our own nine-hole golf course, with little flags to mark the holes. We carved tree limbs out of wood from a cherry tree into the shape of golf clubs and used them to swat the ball. We did that until some of the members of the country club took pity on us and turned over some of their old golf clubs.

3

Q: Golf instructor Stewart Maiden, who taught some of the legends of golf the game, rarely talked theory. His approach to golf was blunt, direct and to the point. For example, when one of his students would question him about his swing or stance, Maiden wouldn't address the question directly. He would tell the person to move closer to the ball, to do this or that. Then he would step back and say, "Okay, now knock the hell out of it." That was the extent of his advice. What do you think of this approach?

A: It works. Tom Bennett, a native of Scotland, golf professional and a greens keeper, was my instructor. He kept hammering away that if I developed a perfect grip, the grip he would teach me, my game would improve dramatically. He said in that wonderful Scottish burr, 'Laddy, if you keep the grip I teach you, you'll never go wrong. Even if your swing isn't perfect, the grip will do the job because it's the main thing to help you hit the ball straight. He lived until I was 22. When he was 66, he came down with cancer of the larynx and it killed him. The final two years of his life, he had to talk with one of those voice boxes. Bennett's son, Jim, was my same age and a lifelong friend. After his father died, Jim took care of all the caddies. Every Monday they would have Caddies Day, and the caddies could play for free. At the beginning, I was too young and too small to play, so they let me compete in a putting contest. I was a pretty good putter even at six and won a gold watch.

(Gen, seated next to Eddie at the table, interrupts: "You never told me that story. Wouldn't it be wonderful if you still had that gold watch? What happened to it?" Eddie shrugs. He doesn't remember. The interview continues.)

4

Q: Most students of the game of golf try to learn everything they can about backspin, club contact and aerodynamics. Golfers feel by proper use of these tools, they can make the ball travel wherever they want it to go. What about backspin and aerodynamics? Your thoughts, please?

A; Well, when I wanted backspin, I used a club with ridges because it would produce backspin and make the ball stop or slow down. If I didn't need it, if I wanted the ball to roll, I would use a club without ridges. The club had the same loft, but it was smooth faced. As for club contact, when you place the ball between your feet, the idea is to hit the ball first and then the turf. That way, you keep the club face in line and force the ball on a straight line to where you're aiming. I never had a problem with aerodynamics. The perfect grip Bennett taught me took care of that.

Q: When I learned to play golf as a caddy at the Yough, I discovered I could get the best distance and the most accuracy by slowing my backswing. My descending stroke would start out slow and accelerate with a terrific punch and follow through that would put my ball far beyond the other golfers in my foursome. From my experience, it seems that most beginning golfers held the club too tightly in their effort to get distance. One legendary golf pro said the average beginning golfer's grip reminded him of someone holding a poisonous snake and being afraid the snake would bite them! Jones was strong on using the three smaller fingers of his left hand to hold the club, then releasing the proper speed of the club head to get maximum distance. How would you approach such a shot?

A: Tom Bennett helped me on this question. My approach, as you call it, was to not grip the club too tightly. I would hold it firm and keep my left arm straight, then follow through with the left arm in position. The speed of the club head would determine the distance and the accuracy of the shot. It worked for me and I think it would work for anyone who follows this formula.

Q; In the early part of the 19th century, there was a Scotchman named S. Mure Ferguson, who was known for his long drives. To any observer, it would appear he was swinging his club so slowly, yet well within himself. And yet when his body uncoiled –

A: Like a snake.

Q: Yes, just like a snake, the ball would sail an incredible distance and wind up in the center of the fairway.

A: It's almost like releasing a projectile, or a rocket. But you have to be very careful not to disturb the balance and the timing of the swing. Otherwise, you'd have a missed shot.

Q: Top golfers have told me they learned as much from making bad shots as making good ones. One also told me golf helped make him into a better person. Has golf helped mold Eddie Rack's character?

A: Absolutely. I would say that it all helps, especially the discipline. Doing the same thing over and over again until it becomes automatic. Your goal is perfection. And you always have to play to win. You'll get beat, but you always play to win, even with your best friends. It's the only way to play the game.

JUST CALL ME LUCKY

THE EDDIE RACK STORY

BY EDDIE RACK
WITH GENO LAWRENZI

CHAPTER ONE

"You look like you could use a little help getting up that hill. Want me to carry you?"

Without waiting for an answer, the golfer picked me up and tucked me under his arm. Then, to my embarrassment, he toted me up the hill on the Youghigheny Country Club's seventh hole, a par three that was one of the toughest holes on the course.

While my face reddened with embarrassment, I could hear my older brother, Victor, snickering with glee. I was just six and this was my first caddying job. The caddy master had given me to Frank Schultz, a first baseman for the McKeesport National Tube, a semi-professional team. Victor, eight, was caddying for his golfing partner, Eddie Trax, a member of the Water Authority and a local politician.

Schultz was tall and muscular, with a good sense of humor. He finally sensed that I wasn't thrilled with his special treatment and put me down, along with the canvas bag that contained his clubs. He winked at me.

"Don't worry, kid," he said. "You're a good caddy. I was just having some fun."

I knew about his baseball team. Frank Schultz was a better golfer than a hitter and would never advance beyond the semi-professional ranks. That day when we came into the 19th hole and I carried his golf bag to his car, he handed me a dollar.

"Mr. Schultz," I stammered, "the fee is only 35 cents…"

"I know," he said. "That's your tip for doing such a good job."

I couldn't believe my good luck, especially when my brother also received a dollar. Our father worked as a coal miner for the Yough 2 Mine in Turkeyfoot, which sat along Route 48. His wages for a day's work amounted to one dollar. That was in the days before John L. Lewis organized the miners into a union and helped upgrade the pay and working conditions for the men who labored long, hard and dangerously beneath the ground.

We ran all the way to our house in Turkey Foot, half a mile away, to give the money to our mother. Both of us were so proud we just stood there with silly grins on our faces. Mom was as astounded as we were.

"Wait til your Dad sees this," said Mom, smiling as she tucked the wrinkled bills into her purse. She gave each of us a big hug. "My little men!"

When Dad came home from work, he was covered with black dust. Wearily he handed his lunch bucket to my mother and took off his hard hat. Only the whites of his eyes and his mouth looked human.

"So what's this I hear about my sons earning all that money?" he said. "You kids earned more than your old man did." He patted me on the head, leaving coal dust on me, and went to wash up.

A dollar doesn't sound like much these days, but in 1919, it was equivalent to a $20 tip. Our oldest brother, Louis, who had just turned 10, was so impressed with our good luck that he joined us at the caddy shack the next day.

The fee for a caddy in 1919 was 15 cents for the first nine holes, and 20 cents for the second nine. Most of the golfers paid 50 cents for the full 18, but there were a few like Schultz and Trax who didn't mind parting with a dollar. My favorite was Capt. Howder, a big strapping man who was a steamboat captain on the Monongahela River. Like many of the other players, Capt. Howder wasn't a very good golfer. He simply played for the fun and relaxation.

In those days, there were very few female players, but the women who did come to the Yough, as we caddies nicknamed it, were always dressed to the hilt. You had to have money to belong to the Yough, and since they came from the best families, they were determined to look stylish. I never saw them on the course without a hat and no woman would be caught dead on the course without a dress. Slacks for women in those days? Forget it. It just didn't happen.

Although I was only six, I was strong for my age and the constant walking up and down the hills carrying a bag of golf clubs helped me develop my leg and chest muscles. After a while, the caddy master decided I was big enough to carry a "double" – two bags that would earn me twice what a single golfer would pay.

The bags weren't like they are today, big expensive leather contraptions with all the amenities. In those days, most of the golfers had a simple white canvas bag. Each bag had six clubs – a driver, brassie or three-wood, mid iron, mashie (five iron), niblick that served as a pitching wedge and a putter.

There was no bus service to the golf course and even if there was, we couldn't afford it. My brothers and I would walk to the Yough, usually arriving around 7 a.m. If you got there any later, you probably wouldn't be called since the parking lot would be filled with caddies of all descriptions and ages and you had to sign in with the caddy master, who picked you on a first come, first out basis. With jobs scarce, the place would be filled with young men in their late teens or early twenties.

If my brothers and I arrived late and there was a big list, we would walk to the wooded area along number 10 or number four and look for golf balls. The woods were thick and golfers were always hooking or slicing a shot into the trees. The golfers and their caddies would spend a certain amount of time looking for a lost ball. When they failed to find it, which was often the case, they would leave it there, drop another ball and continue their game.

Finding a shiny new ball was always a thrill because it meant money in our pockets.

Years later, I would tell people we were always on the lookout for golf balls. I would add, only half jokingly, "Sometimes we didn't even wait for it to stop rolling before we had it in our pocket!

On number four, one of my favorite holes, the fairway ran parallel to the Mt. Vernon Cemetery. That was one of the best places to look for lost balls. For some reason, the golfers were reluctant to walk across the road to search for their errant shot. People would be there paying respects to departed relatives or friends, or laying flowers next to the stone markers.

That didn't bother the Rack boys.

There were times a funeral was in session a short distance away. We didn't mean any disrespect for the dead, but if I spotted a shiny white ball next to a tombstone, I was there in a flash, knowing I could sell it for up to 25 cents if it was in good condition.

Each Monday morning was Caddies Day. That was the day any caddy that wanted to could play for free on the Yough, which was, and still is, one of the finest country clubs in Pennsylvania. Hardly any of the caddies was rich enough to afford his own clubs, so we had to rely on the generosity of a friendly golfer to lend us his clubs. Since I was so small, the caddy master wouldn't allow me to play. However, he did set up a regular putting competition. I practiced my putting regularly, usually while standing in the woods along the fairway while my golfer and his companions walked up the hill to tee off. After a while, I got so good that I won a gold watch in the putting contest.

My first golf club was made out of a limb from a cherry tree. Cherry was a soft wood, easy to carve with the penknife I always carried. Louis, Victor and I each cut out a club from cherry wood. We also built our own nine-hole golf course near our house and began practicing our shots.

Although my brothers were fairly good golfers, they didn't take the same interest in the game that I did. Despite my age, I could always beat them on a regular basis. Later when I joined the McKeesport High School golf team, my game improved to the point that they gave up trying to beat me and turned to other sports. Louis was an outstanding baseball player for the Boston Bulldogs, while Vic turned into one of the best tackles in the area, playing football for the McKeesport Olympics, Christie Park Panthers, Versailles Crescents and the Bryn Mawr Bulldogs. He stood six-two and weighed about 240 pounds. Louis was five-ten and tipped the scales at 200. I was five-eleven and weighed about the same as Louis.

The other caddies were aggressive and fun loving. There were the usual number of challenges and fights, and they loved to gamble when they weren't out on a job. They pitched pennies against a building and sometimes played cards behind the shack where the caddy master and greens keeper stored their equipment. I never had to worry about fighting. My big brother, Vic, took care of my fights for me and everybody knew it, so they left me alone.

Looking back on those days, I can find myself smiling. Even though we were poor and never had much in the way of luxuries, it was about as close to a perfect childhood as you could find. The camaraderie, being with my brothers, the proud feeling of being able to earn money to help at home were things I will remember as long as I live. Even today, I find myself thinking about it and it brings a warm feeling to me that someone who hasn't done it will never understand.

The caddy master was boss and we thought of him as a kind of god. "Eddie," he would snap, sticking his head out the door and looking at me. "You're caddying for Dr. Ritchie. He's on the putting green and he'll start on number ten. Get moving!"

His order would be enough to launch me like a rocket. Feeling important as the adrenalin shot through my system, I would scurry up to the caddy shack, grab the clubs and throw them over my skinny shoulder. We caddies developed a way to carry a set of clubs that was all our own. I would put my left arm and elbow over the club heads, and swing the bag behind my body so I was leaning into the clubs. They felt lighter that way and gave me balance as I trudged up inclines or into valleys to find my golfer's ball. Even today I can always tell a former caddy by the way he carries his clubs. It's something you never forget.

BOB SHERMAN, EDDIE RACK'S SON-IN-LAW AND ASSISTANT MANAGER AT 7 SPRINGS:

How can I describe my father-in-law? Lucky, lucky, lucky. Probably the most generous man you would ever want to meet. If he wins, everybody wins.

15

CHAPTER TWO

I was just four years old when my parents decided to leave a farm in Wisconsin, where we had been living and move to western Pennsylvania. I don't remember much about living on the farm. My childhood memories begin near the Palisades where we made our new home.

My father told me later that he couldn't earn a decent living working on the farm. That was the deciding factor that made him and my mother move. He found a job working in the mines and my mother cleaned floors. We were very poor.

Victor, Louis and I soon found jobs selling the McKeesport Daily news on the streets of the bustling steel and coal city. We would buy the newspapers for a penny and sell them for a 100 per cent profit. You can see I became an entrepreneur at an early age! The city council had a 9 p.m. curfew when anyone under the age of 16 had to be off the streets. A cop in our neighborhood enforced it. My brothers and I would hide until he passed by, then we would go out and hawk newspapers until all of them were sold.

Dad worked in a mine beneath Turkeyfoot Road, about a mile from our home. We were living in Turkey Foot, a coal mining patch, when my brothers and I enrolled at the Boston School in the Knights of Pythias Building. After I reached my sixth birthday, I decided to step up in the world and find a better job, just like my Dad had done.

Back then, Youghiogheny Country Club was just nine holes. Some of my school mates caddied there after school and on weekends. They said the work wasn't that hard and the money was easy, so my brothers and I paid the club a visit. We were hired as caddies almost immediately, although the caddy master took a long look at me before he decided to let me go to work. He muttered something about me not being "much bigger than a golf bag," but he gave me a chance. I'll always be grateful for his wise decision.

I made a lot of friends among the caddies, including several people who would become lifelong friends, like Bill Peckman and William Pigozzi, who later graduated from medical school and became a well-known doctor in the area. Caddying is a tough job, as anyone who has caddied for pay will tell you. Walking up and down those hills, keeping an eye on the ball and staying in line with your golfer requires serious effort and dedication. My legs were short compared to the other caddies and those long strides of the golfers made me hustle to keep pace. Most of the golfers were good natured about the little kid with their canvas bag strapped to his back. After a while, my leg muscles had developed to the point where I could keep up with them.

As I grew older, I tried some other jobs, but I always seemed to go back to caddying. When I graduated from the eighth grade, for example, I spent the summer working as a concrete finisher for John Butler, who built Rock Run Road. The work was hard, hot and humid, but he paid me 25 cents an hour. I decided to go back to the golf course.

One of the strongest influences in my life was W.D. Mansfield, a Pennsylvania State Senator and publisher of the McKeesport Daily News. Mr. Mansfield had a standing 7 a.m. tee time at the Yough. He would play a quick nine holes in less than an hour, literally making the caddies run to keep up with him, and be in his office at the Daily News by 8 a.m. I was always happy when I got to carry his bag.

I didn't get my first golf clubs until the age of 12. My clubs until then consisted of hand-carved limbs from cherry trees and some old clubs with wooden shafts that the golfers had thrown away. Some of those clubs were so useless I had to replace the shaft with a new one. I didn't mind the work. My interest in playing golf was always serious and I wanted the best possible clubs I could afford, which in those days was next to nothing.

When somebody asks me where I got my drive to succeed, I give the credit to my mother, the former Mary Volk. My father died in a tragic mining accident (more about that later) when I was just 10 years old after fathering three sons and a daughter. Mom died at the age of 79 after working hard all of her life. She was the one who held the purse strings in the family. A native of Yugoslavia, she had come to America at the age of 16. My father was also born in Yugoslavia. Both of them could speak the language of their homeland.

Mom never threw anything away.

She had a no-nonsense attitude toward life and would save anything that came into our home, figuring there must be a use for it. I usually saw the stern side of her, but she also had a gentle side. After Gen and I had gotten married, my mother came over for a visit. Gen was in the finishing stages of tidying up our small place and Mom saw her saving slivers of soap.

"Good," said Mom, nodding her head approvingly. "I like that."

Mom learned to read English by looking over the books my siblings and I brought home from school. She would pore over them for hours, pretending to help us with our homework, but we all knew she was secretly studying the words and practicing her English. It still touches me today in a special way when I think of how she stuck to her task.

Because of her desire to learn, Mom became very knowledgeable about this country and she grew into an excellent reader. She eventually became a naturalized citizen. My father never did, even though he loved living in America.

Money was so hard to come by in those days that I treated it like it was gold. While other caddies pitched pennies, I watched, joining in only when somebody pushed me into it. I thought it was dumb to throw away your money on a chance that you might win somebody's penny.

One game I did engage in with enthusiasm was playing marbles. We all had our bag of marbles with a "shooter" – a big heavy marble that you could use to knock the other kids' marbles out of the pot and win them. The best shooters were the ones we called steelies. They were made of steel and came from the steel mills, where some of my friends' fathers worked. If you had a steelie, you developed a definite edge and your sack of marbles would get bigger and bigger. I can't remember ever being without my share of marbles from the time I was eight until I was in my teens. In fact, when I was in the eighth grade, I actually won a marble shooting competition for the eighth grader division held at the Young Men's Christian Association. The American Legion presented me with a trophy and took my picture.

My brothers and I always got along well. Because of my size, they were very protective of me. When we would have a pick-up baseball game, I was too small to play, but they would let me collect the tickets. We charged people a quarter to watch the game and used the proceeds to buy baseballs or bats.

Our games were held at the Boston Ball Field beneath the Boston Bridge. Sometimes we would start a game between two rival teams with a single ball and two bats that both teams shared. If the ball would separate because of the heavy pounding, someone would dig out the heavy black masking tape to keep the baseball from unraveling. We played against all the area teams – Boston, Blythedale, Sutersville, Christie Park and Scott Haven. One of the great Negro teams of the era, the Homestead Grays, played on our field. They had some excellent ball players, men who could have been major leaguers if blacks had been permitted to play with the professionals. Such a process had been long overdue but it would come later, thanks to the determination of people like Jackie Robinson and Branch Rickey.

When I was a sophomore in high school, I discovered I had a problem with my vision. I was walking down the street when a best friend on the other side of the street waved at me and yelled, "Hi, Eddie." I didn't recognize him. I told my mother about it and she scheduled an appointment with an optometrist. After an exam, he told me, "You need glasses." I've worn them ever since.

Through my teens, I turned into a long distance driver and my putting improved to the point that I became competitive with the other caddies. Some of the country club members like Doc Kelly (his first name was Clarence, but we never used that name when we referred to him) took an interest in me in more ways than one. One morning – I was 16 years old – I caddied 36 holes. The last 18 I was Doc Kelly's caddy.

On the backside, my stomach began hurting. The doctor noticed I was in pain and came over to me.

"What's wrong, son?" he inquired kindly. "You don't look so good."

"It's nothing, Doc," I said. "Just a little indigestion I guess."

He shook his head. "I don't know about that. Listen, you go home and take some citrate of magnesia. Don't worry about finishing the round. I'll pay you what I owe you. But if you don't improve, you come by my office, now, you hear?" I said I did, and promised to take his advice.

The next morning, my stomach was puffed up like a balloon. My mother took one look, told me to get dressed and she took me to his office. After an examination, he put his stethoscope in a case and gave me a long look. Then he turned to my mother.

"He has appendicitis," the doctor said. "I have to operate."

"When will the operation be?" my mother wanted to know.

"As soon as possible."

The surgery was completed the same day and I came out of it in fine shape except for a big red scar. Doc Kelly knew my family had no money to pay him. He put it on the books and never sent us a bill.

After I started working at the Daily News, I paid Doc Kelly an unannounced visit. Ten years had passed since the emergency operation. I walked into his office and he smiled in recognition.

"Doc, remember when you took out my appendicitis?"

"Sure do, Eddie. You were a good patient."

"Thanks, Doc. I don't think my family ever paid you. I came by today to settle up."

The good physician rose from behind his desk. He smiled and said, "Eddie, I wrote that off the books a long time ago. You don't owe me a cent. You were always one of my favorite caddies."

When I left his office that day, my eyes brimmed with tears, just like they're doing right now just thinking of that fine man. Gen has some great memories of Doc Kelly, too. After we were married, Gen and I traveled to New York City. She came down with a bad infection, probably caused by a mosquito bite. Gen said it felt like a carbuncle and really hurt. She thought she might have scratched it to cause an infection. Anyhow, she called Doc Kelly and set up an appointment. He cut it out and took care of it. His son, Frank, became a close friend of my son, Norm, who was just 16 when he won the title of champion of the Youghiogheny Country Club. A few years passed. Norm was kind of loafing around and playing golf, with no real job prospects in mind. He had graduated from high school and was considered one of the Yough's top golfers, but nothing seemed to be happening for him.

Three years later, Frank called Norm and me into his office, where he operated his own photography business. He said to me, 'Eddie, I think Norm has a real future on the tour. I am willing to give him $30,000 to cover his expenses for the next two years, if you and your son agree.

"If he does well, he can pay me back – but that is not a requisite. What do you say?"

Norm looked at me and then he looked at Frank and shook his hand. "It's a deal," he said. That is the kind of family the Kellys are. You don't find any better people than that. If I ever failed to include the Kelly family in my prayers, shame on me. Shame on me!

CHAPTER THREE

In 1935, I received my diploma and graduated from McKeesport High School. But if it hadn't been for W.D. Mansifield, it would never have happened.

Money was always a big concern in the Rack family and our economic situation grew worse after my father's death. My brothers and I took our family responsibilities seriously and were constantly looking for new ways to be the "man" in the family. That meant earning enough money to pay the bills.

I liked caddying for a number of reasons. It was a healthy outdoor job that kept me out of trouble and kept the dollars flowing into my pockets. It pleased me to no end to be able to come home at the end of a day, tired but satisfied, and hand my mother a fistful of bills and change, the pay for my labor. School wasn't really that exciting for me. My grades were passable but not outstanding. When school was in session, I had to crack the books and do homework, which cut into the hours I could spend on the golf course.

Since golf was becoming such a big part of my life, I came up with an idea I thought would help the situation at home and at the same time give me more time to play golf: I would drop out of school and become a full-time caddy like some of the other guys had done.

Somehow the word got back to Mr. Mansfield. One day he called me aside for a man-to-man talk.

"Eddie, what's this I hear about you wanting to become a high school drop-out?" he said.

I hung my head, a bit embarrassed. I couldn't avoid his direct look and finally had to face him.

"It's true, Mr. Mansfield. My family could use the money and I want to improve my game. School isn't that important for me –"

"Maybe school isn't, but an education is," he interjected. "As you get older, you'll understand that a lot better. I know what it's like not to have money and I can sympathize with you. I'll tell you what. On the day you graduate from high school and show me your diploma, I'll give you a job working for my newspaper."

My heart started beating faster. I didn't know what to say. Finally I managed to stammer, "You'd do that for me?"

"Absolutely, Eddie. I'm a man of my word. But remember this: no diploma, no job! Do we have a deal?"

We shook hands. We had a deal.

I concentrated on my studies and my grades began improving. I even developed a liking for school, although the golf course was still my favorite place to hang out. Mansfield would ask me how things were going from time to time, and I always gave him an honest answer.

The high school had a golf team, probably one of the best in the state, and I became a member. I played on the team from 1932 to the year I graduated, winning club championships at a number of area golf courses, including Butler's, Baldoc, Irwin and the Yough. As a representative of the printer's union, I won 11 of 13 national typographical tournaments. My name began appearing regularly in the sports pages of the McKeesport Daily News, where the writers took an interest in me. One of the highlights of my high school golf days was winning permanent possession of the Walter Hagen Trophy after a third victory in the Union Printers Invitational Golf Association Tournament near Washington D.C. Even while I was winning those early tournaments, I was making life-long friends who would make a huge difference in my life in the future.

I graduated on a Sunday. The following morning, I went to the Daily News and a secretary ushered me into Mr. Mansfield's office to tell him I was reporting to work.

"Calling my bluff, are you?" He smiled and congratulated me on winning my diploma.

"I'm going to make a typesetter out of you," he said. "The starting salary is $12 a week. You'll have to fill out an application to join the typographical union, but that won't be a problem. You need to be an apprentice before you become a printer."

My work went well and the other printers went

out of their way to show me the ropes. The union had formed its own golf league and I began playing tournaments as a representative of the union. It didn't hurt that the union stewards knew the publisher of the newspaper was my mentor.

That year I took the most important step of my life. I met the woman who was to become my wife and life-long companion.

I loved to dance and a Friday night dance was scheduled at the Whoopee Club, a popular social club in Pigeon Hollow. The dance floor was just a platform made of planks. They didn't have a live band, but a Victrola supplied the music. All of the males pitched in to buy a keg of beer and soft drinks for the ladies who didn't like alcohol.

My sister was responsible for introducing me to Genevieve Davis. If it wasn't love at first sight, it was close to it. Genevieve (I shortened her name to Gen because it was easier to say) lived just down the road in Boston. She turned out to be the prettiest girl in the place as well as the best dancer. She agreed to dance with me, and we glided across the floor. I felt like Heaven had come down and was looking me in the face. From that moment on, we were practically inseparable. I didn't want to let her go and when I escorted her back to her friends, I said, "You're going to be seeing a lot of me!" Her response of "I'd like that," made my heart take a little leap.

Gen and I became a couple, as they say, and by summer I realized I had fallen in love. Fortunately for me, she felt the same way. When I asked her to marry me, she said yes. On Nov. 29, 1935, we became husband and wife. I wasted no time in going before Mr. Mansfield and asking for a raise, pointing out I had taken on a new responsibility. He pursed his lips, nodded and said, "How does $14 a week sound?" I had been hoping for more but said it was fine. This was 1935, remember, and a buck went a long way. Now I had to face a much more serious problem: convincing my mother that Gen and I needed the money more than she did!

At first she stubbornly refused to even consider it. My brothers and sisters came to my rescue, arguing, "Mom, he's married and has to support a wife." Finally, and with great reluctance, she made the concession. It didn't take long for Gen to make a big impression on Mom and they eventually became the best of friends.

Golf is a game that requires your constant attention for you to play well enough to win, especially in a tournament situation. I was deadly serious about my game. When I wasn't working at the Daily News, I was either on the golf course or the putting green, testing all the techniques to make my game more perfect. Although I played at all of the golf courses in a 100-mile radius of my home, my favorite was and still is the Youghiogheny Country Club, and that includes all the golf courses I have ever played. I recommend it to any serious student of the game.

In 1950 at South Hills Country Club, I tried to qualify for the U.S. Open. There were 120 professionals and amateurs trying for eight spots, and the competition was formidable. When the play was finished, nine pros and an amateur had qualified by shooting 141 for two rounds. I shot a 70 in my opening round and a 71 in the second, playing all 36 holes without a three-putt.

With nine qualifiers and only eight open spots, we had to play off on the number one hole. I hit the green in two shots and, unbelievably, had my first three-putt of the tournament!

It happened this way. I putted the ball two and a half feet from the hole and missed it for a bogie. Six of the golfers shot par and two others, like me, had a five, requiring the three of us to play one hole. Two of us would make the Open and the third would go home. The hole was a 600-yard par five and I have to tell you I was beside myself with excitement.

Lionel Hebert and Willie Beljan made pars while I three putted and wound up with a heart-breaking six. Ten years later at Oakmont Country Club, Lionel spotted me and hurried over to shake my hand.

"Eddie Rack," he said quietly. "You know, if you hadn't three-putted on number one, my whole life could have changed." That three-putt sent him on his way to win a lot of major golf tournaments. Up to that point, he had served as assistant pro at Oakmont and had actually been considering giving up on the tour. After making the cut, he never returned to Oakmont.

Well, I went back home and the qualifiers went on to Texas. I had a wife and three children at the time, and Lionel was a bachelor. It was meant to be and I accepted it. What else can you do?

On one other occasion, I nearly qualified for the U.S. Open. That day I shot a 70 at Baldoc Hills Country Club, two under par. I was still two under after 10 holes at Greensburg Country Club. My son, Norm, went over to the leader board. He was 10 years old and caddying for me. He came over excitedly.

"Dad, if you bogy all the way in, you can still make the cut," he said, trying, I guess, to give me confidence. It had the exact opposite effect. I bogied six of the final eight holes and missed the cut by a single stroke. Norm, when you read this, I love you son and I'm not blaming you. That was just the way it turned out. It wasn't meant to be.

I started telling you about the Youghiogheny Country Club. This beautiful golf course and country club was founded in 1911 on a tract of farm land once owned by Col. William Douglas. It began life as a four-hole course with a renovated farm house as the social center. The golf enthusiasts who decided to take a hand in expanding it were W.A. Cornelius, who later was elected president; J. Audley Pierce; W.D. Mansfield, my employer, mentor and friend; Dr. G.P. Gamble; A.W. Powell; Thomas Fox; and A.M. Saunders.

Before it was converted into a golf course, the property was simply known as the McClure farm. Col. Douglas was a man of many faces. He was a pioneer, property owner, public official and banker. Four generations of his family lived in the old homestead. Before he died in 1876, he willed the homestead, consisting of rich rolling fields and natural scenic surroundings, to his son and daughter. After that, the property passed on to Alexander McClure and his heirs.

The golfers purchased the 107 acres for $9,250. They held their first meeting of record to organize the country club on Feb. 8, 1911, with 14 men present. They chose the Indian name, Youghiogheny, which means "River of many bends," and financed the club by selling bonds to the membership.

On April 10, 1911, a meeting of subscribers to the country club was held at the main office of U.S. Steel Corporation's National Works. Mansfield had a significant say in determining the direction of the club and remained in a leadership position at the Yough for the rest of his life.

Youghiogheny Country Club opened its doors officially on Memorial Day, May 30, 1911. The members had added two more holes and it remained that way until 1913, when the front nine was completed on the original 107 acres.

As the years passed and the club's membership grew, major improvements were made, including a spacious porch around the building and a large dining room. Baseball was the craze in those days, and the men started a baseball team, which lasted less than a year. They also constructed tennis courts and a gun club with traps on the country club property. It must have been interesting for a golf foursome to be coming in on a hole, only to see puffs of smoke and the sounds of shotguns going off a short distance away.

The members held regular shooting competitions until 1928 when the gun club was disbanded. Mansfield, a shooting enthusiast, re-established trap shooting on the property the same year, but it ended after the start of World War II.

When the second nine holes were completed. Taylor Alderdice, a former superintendent of National Works who later became president of National Tube Co., was given the honor of hitting the first ball. His foursome included S. M. Lynch, John A. Caughey and George Duncan. I caddied for Mr. Duncan.

Today the terrace dining room, which opened its doors in 1952, is a favorite stopping place for the members. The dining room is on the open porch facing the number one tee and you could not ask for a more scenic view. An Olympic-sized swimming pool was added to the property in 1954 and four years later, the course was piped for water to nourish the fairways and greens. The friendly grille room, a favorite with the membership, was completed in 1960.

I have to smile when I think of how little it cost the members to join in those early days. The initiation fee was $50, with annual dues of $25.

Today the country club sits on 235 of the best acres in Pennsylvania. Even William Penn, who nicknamed the state "Penn's Woods," would have to be proud of it. Nobody can walk or ride a cart over those 18 holes, with the magnificent trees, fairways and shrubbery, without being impressed. If you ever have an opportunity to play there, I promise the memory will stay with you forever, as it has for the Rack family. The only thing I regret is the fact that the caddies have been replaced with electric golf carts. I realize you can't hold back progress, but it still pains my heart and saddens me that the era of caddies has passed and I'll never hear the caddy master yell, "Boy!...Dr. Piggozi is on the putting green. He'll start on the back nine. Get his bag..."

LOU SPOSATO, OWNER OF A CADILLAC DEALERSHIP IN WHITEHALL, PA. AND A LONG-TIME FRIEND OF THE RACKS:

I met Eddie around 1956 when I drove over

to 7 Springs to play a round of golf. At the time I was general manager of a car dealership and wanted to see what there was about this game that was attracting all my friends. I was a pretty poor player, but my cousin and I started playing there on a regular basis.

One day Eddie came around to our table and we began talking. The outcome of that was Eddie buying a new Cadillac from me. I discovered Eddie liked to gamble a little. He played blackjack and gin. I was a dice player who liked poker.

We started going to Atlantic City and Las Vegas. I was considered the high roller, and Eddie just came along for fun. We always got the royal treatment, including complimentary room, meals, drinks and shows.

Here is what I found out about Eddie from all those trips. The man has a horseshoe up his – well, you know the word. I won't say it. Ladies or children might be reading this and I don't want to offend anybody.

When Eddie is playing gin, after seven cards are on the board, he knows what you have in your hand! The man has a photographic memory, even at the age of 90. Unless you have a no-brainer hand, he's going to beat you.

We flew to Las Vegas to watch the Tyson-Holyfield fight, the one where Big Mike bit off part of Holyfield's ear. When the fight ended, because of the way it ended, there was a riot at the MGM Grand. We had to inch our way out of the place. I remember worrying about Eddie. The man was almost 90 years old and I thought something could happen to him. Hah! I'm the one I should have been worried about. We went out the back way, started down an incline and he beat me to the bottom.

The next day I started shooting dice and Eddie played blackjack. I was down maybe $1,300 and he was losing around $500. I said, let's go and have some lunch. He said okay, but let me finish out this shoe first. When the shoe was finished, we headed for the restaurant. As we were passing a clean-up man who looked like he had seen better days, Eddie flips him a quarter chip.

"Eddie," I says, "that's a green chip. Twenty-five bucks. What are you doing?"

He looks at me and says, "Lou, we're lucky we're still walking. If God wanted you to keep money, he'd have put handles on it."

The Eddie Rack family, shown here, owns stock in both corporations. Edward Rack Inc. owns Colony West Country Club Inc. 7 Springs Inc., is debt-free, Rack proudly points out, and all the outstanding shares are owned by the nine family stock holders. From left, standing: Lynne Behelar, Mark Kuehner, Dale Kuehner, Craig Rack and Tracy Marcello. Seated from left: Janice Sherman, Genevieve Rack, Edward Rack and Norman Rack.

CHAPTER FOUR

Joining the Typographical Union and representing the union in amateur tournaments all over the country was one of the best things that ever happened to me. It was like being part of one large family, and W.D. Mansfield was the father. I eventually became a member of the Youghigheny Country Club, a position I held for many years, and that was good, too. When you belong to a country club and you become club champ, not once but several times, people begin to talk about you. It helps build your stature, makes people notice and it builds your name. That old show business song, "Life is a Cabaret" pretty well sums up the way I felt.

One of the most influential men I have ever met was Bill Sullivan. He would play a key role into turning me into a millionaire golf course owner and it all began because I caddied for him.

Sullivan was a member at the Yough. For some reason, he and I hit it off well and he began asking for me when he showed up to play a round of golf. He, along with Mansfield, urged me to stay in school. He also encouraged me to join the golf team at McKeesport High, where he was the head coach. The team's home course was the Yough, which meant I could practice there whenever I wanted, as long as it didn't interfere with my caddying duties. My fellow golf team members included Crawford Kelly, Peden Gamble, Aldo Zecchini and two young men who would become future physicians, Dr. Ritchie and Dr. Caughey.

I began playing the country club circuit and started understanding what the good life was all about. Ever see that movie, "Sabrina," starring Audrey Hepburn, William Holden and Humphrey Bogart. Wonderful film, one of my favorites. Gen loves it, too. Anyhow, that was the sort of life I was living after winning the championship at Indiana Country Club and the Greater Johnstown Amateur Championship. My putting even got me to the finals of the West Penn Amateurs. And the biggest honor of all came when I played with a legend named Arnold Palmer at a Yough Exhibition for the McKeesport Rotary Club.

Arnold was slim, self-assured and wonderful. Even now, half a century later, I can see him stepping up to the green, his ball eight feet from the hole. Dropping his cigarette on the fringe. Stepping up to the ball with a cool detachment you felt rather than saw, and ramming the ball into the hole. Incredible. And I not only witnessed it, I played against him – and beat the great Arnold Palmer. I shot a 69 against Arnold's 71. As we walked to the 19th hole, Palmer turned toward me with a smile and winked.

"I'll get you, Rack," he said softly. "Remember that." And he did exactly that a few years later.

Sullivan had become a successful township real estate developer. He took a flyer on some wooded farmland, feeling it could be turned into a golf course.

One day he called me aside for a conference.

"Ed, I want you to take a look at a piece of property I just bought," he said. "Tell me what you think of it. I want to develop it into a golf course."

I went with him to his acquisition and was immediately impressed. The wooded rolling land was adjacent to Route 51, a major highway leading into Pittsburgh, and Route 48, a country road that connected with a number of nearby communities. I thought it was perfect for a golf course and told that to Sullivan.

He asked me to help him lay out the course, and we did it together, all 18 holes. Sullivan was the expert, but I gave him my input and he was a good listener. The course opened officially on May 13, 1955 as 7 Springs Golf Course.

Shortly after the opening, Sullivan asked me if I would consider managing it for him.

"I'm too busy with other projects to do it myself, Ed," he told me. "I think you have the energy and know how to do a good job of running it. If you come up short, I'll be there to help you."

The project sounded almost too big for me, even though I was a pretty confident young man. But this one?

Genevieve gives a warm hug to her son, Scoop. He was born Edward Kent Rack on Aug., 1936, and died of complications from diabetes and kidney failure at age 62.

Eddie and Gen Rack relax in the Fairway Room at Colony West Country Club, Tamarac, FL. on New Year's Eve, 2002.

The affection between Eddie and Gen Rack is plain
for all to see as the couple cuddle up in front of Hole
One at 7 Springs Golf Course.

Eddie Rack, the pro shows amateur golfer and co-
author Geno Lawrenzi Jr. the perfect golf grip.

Genevieve, Eddie and great-grandson, Ian,
at home in 7 Springs.

"I don't know, Mr. Sullivan," I said hesitantly. "I'll talk it over with my wife."

Gen called our children into the family conference. By that time, we had three – Eddie, Janice and 10-year-old Norman.

"Well, what do you kids think?" Gen said. "Will you help Daddy run a golf course?"

The enthusiasm of my wife and our children decided the issue for me. I agreed to give it the old college try.

There was a major problem, of course, and one I had to think about long and hard before going ahead. Once I opened a golf shop, I could no longer play as an amateur. I told Sullivan I would take the job and applied for membership in the Tri-State PGA. That turned out to be an incredible move for me. Over a 10-year period (1965-75), I served twice as tournament director and was elected to the positions of secretary-treasurer and president.

A year later, Sullivan gave me another call.

"Eddie, I'm going to get married," he said.

"That's wonderful. Congratulations."

"I want to move to Florida and start developing property down there, Ed," Sullivan continued, as though he hadn't heard me.

"But what about 7 Springs?"

"I've been thinking about that. How would you like to buy the golf course?"

If he had hit me between the eyes with a two-by-four, he couldn't have stunned me more. I was too shocked to answer him. All I could do was stare him in the eye, feeling like somebody had hooked me up to a hot wire.

"You can do it, Son," he said quietly. "I've watched you. Talk it over with your wife and your family, and then give me your answer. I figure I've invested around $200,000 in the property. All I want is a 20 per cent return on my money. Think you can afford that?"

When good luck comes, you have to recognize it. Sullivan was offering to sell me a valuable, money-making piece of property for $240,000. I promised to get back to him, to look and act calm even though inside I was boiling like a volcano about to erupt.

Although she was in my corner, Gen was nervous about this one, pointing out it would be a tremendous undertaking, not to mention a risky one. I decided to go to the man who had started me out on my career as a golfer – W. D. Mansfield. Besides being publisher of the McKeesport Daily News, he was president of the First National Bank of McKeesport. Mansfield listened to my story with interest. He occasionally nodded, folded and refolded his hands and never took his eyes off me. Finally he picked up the phone and called one of his assistants.

"I have a young man here who needs a loan," he said. "Talk to him. See what we can do."

The rest of the morning went by in a daze. But when I walked out of the First National Bank, I had a check for $240,000. My payment terms were incredibly generous. The bank agreed to accept monthly payments of $340.

The son of an immigrant coal miner now owned a golf course. The Rack dynasty had begun.

DALE KUEHNER'S RECOLLECTIONS:

My grandfather, Eddie Rack, has always been a driving force in my life. He instilled a love of golf in me, not only for the game but also for the beauty of the course. This is what influenced me from a very early age to want to pursue a career as a golf course superintendent.

Over the years I have looked at my grandfather's accomplishments with pride and awe. I wanted to try to emulate some of them myself. Since my golf skills nowhere near compares to his, I tried to emulate his work in the PGA. I joined the South Florida GCSA in 1985 and in 1990 became a member of the South Florida board.

After three years as the South Florida representative, I was elected to the Florida GCSA executive board and became president of the South Florida GCSA in 1996. A year later, I was elected president of the organization and in 1996, I became the voting delegate for the entire state of Florida for the GCSA, a position I proudly hold today.

My grandfather's mantra – give back to those who got you there – has been the main force that drives me to volunteer my time and energy to the superintendent's association. My grandfather has always believed in helping others who are less fortunate than me, and this is why Colony West has hosted the South Florida GCSA's tournament to benefit the Center for Missing and Abused Children. The tournament has been a success and has raised more than $100,000 in the past 10 years.

CRAIG EDWARD RACK'S RECOLLECTIONS:

I am the third of five grandchildren and the youngest grandson in the Rack family. My middle name is named after my grandfather. Growing up, I had many fond memories of my grandfather, many of which I shall never forget. He is one of the kindest men I have ever known, always giving without expectation of receiving. He gave me the opportunity to live, work and enjoy life in the golfing industry. It's a gift I will never take lightly.

Grandpap always has a smile and says "Hi," and makes it a point to shake everyone's hand. You don't forget a person like that. He taught me the importance of being responsible when I was a teenager, by offering the driving range to his grandkids as a business for us to run. Believe me, we took that responsibility seriously. He taught me to work hard, to do the job right, adding, "Someday it will be yours. I have always tried to do that and plan to pass it on to my own children.

The main thing I enjoy most is that almost every day when I go to work, I can see my grandfather. There are three generations of the Rack family out there working. Three generations playing golf, working on the golf courses and playing cards. It doesn't get any better than that. Our family is one of a kind and my grandparents are the ones who kept it together over the years, even when economic times were bad. A family is the one thing you have throughout your life. That is the legacy my grandfather has given to all of us, and that is something I can never forget.

CHAPTER FIVE:

Genevieve Rack's Personal Recollections:

I am the oldest of five children born to Clarence and Helen Davis. My parents were living on Belle Bridge Hill near Port Vue when I was born on Feb. 26, 1915. I grew up with my three sisters, Elinor Grace, Doris Jean and Lila Lee, the baby of the family until my brother, Milton Dale, whom we nicknamed Mooney, was born on Aug. 8, 1935.

Mooney was more like a son than a brother to me, as he was only a few months old when I got married and left home. Our first son, Eddie Kent, was born almost a year to the day after Mooney, and they were always close. My son, Scoop, called him Uncle Mooney Gal. When Mooney died suddenly in 1981 from a heart attack, Scoop was devastated, as we all were.

Our family lived in several places during our early years. I have many fond memories of my grandparents,

William and Sarah Hankins, and my aunts Flo, Jean and Mildred, while we went to live with them in Connellsville near Uniontown. Work was so scarce in those days that Dad would move us from place to place trying to find a steady job. We finally settled down in Pigeon Hollow, where Anne Rack and I became close friends.

Ed and I met at a picnic on Labor Day, 1932. Friends of Ed's and his brothers had built a platform back of their home in Pigeon Hollow, where they danced to old records played on a windup Victrola. Anne Rack and I were friends through school and she knew I loved to dance. One night she invited me to join a bunch of friends, including her three brothers, to listen to records and dance at the Whoopee Club. She added, 'You might even like one of my brothers.'

I got permission from my parents to go to the club, which wasn't far from our house. I remember walking up the hill and hearing the music and laughter. We weren't there very long when Ed came up and asked me to dance. We danced very well together, and he was so nice and thoughtful that when he asked if I would wait for him while he went home to do a chore for his mother, I agreed. It wasn't long before he returned and he looked so delighted to see I had waited for him. We danced the rest of the evening and he walked me home. Our lives together started at that point. Ed always made me feel as though I was very precious to him, and that feeling exists today, making me a very happy woman.

He would walk to my house on weekends and we would swing on our front porch and listen to my father play the mandolin. We didn't have money for movies or going out to eat, but any chance we could, we would go dancing. I remember one of our favorite songs was 'Tea for Two.' We often went to Olympia Park in Versailles, where they held dances in a pavilion featuring such big name bands as Lawrence Welk. Kennywood Park also had live bands to dance to, and we went there often. Ed has always had his golf, but dancing has been our special recreation to this day. In 1948, we were thrilled to win a dance contest at the Yough, dancing to Wayne King. We also traveled to Atlantic City to see Louie Prima and Keely Smith and dance to their music.

Ed and I were very much in love and we knew we would eventually marry, but money was scarce and I never gave a thought to having a big wedding. We asked our friends, Hilda and Frank Hackett, if they would stand for us, and they agreed. We drove to East McKeesport on Nov. 29, 1935, and were married in the parish of Rev. Shane. After the ceremony, the four of us went for dinner to the Star Restaurant on Fifth Avenue in McKeesport. After dinner, we watched a movie at the old Memorial Theater, "A Star is Born," starring Charley Farrell and Janet Gaynor.

After our wedding, we moved into three little rooms that adjoined Ed's family home. We were poor but in love, and we were ecstatic when we learned I was pregnant. Edward Kent, whom we nicknamed Scoop, was born Aug. 6, 1936 at home. He came into the world three weeks early and was a very small baby. In those days, women didn't go to the hospital to have babies, but Dr. Helsel was called and he delivered our first son.

Scoop was a beautiful child, but we soon noticed he wasn't developing as quickly as he should. Doctors didn't have the medical knowledge then to diagnose Scoop, but we discovered later he had Willy's Prader Syndrome. It hindered his normal development, but not his personality or his voice. Scoop loved country music and Hank Williams was one of his favorites. He carried a tune well and we always enjoyed hearing him sing.

Gambling has always been a part of Ed's life. His family loved to get together to play cards and his mother had her favorites – Fan Tan and Crazy Eights. Although I was raised to believe that gambling was sin and the "Work of the Devil," I saw how much Ed enjoyed it, and that made me happy. Ed had a group of friends, Duane Layton, Harold Ball, Frank Gerschaut and some others, who took turns hosting card games at their homes. I always told him, 'Ed, I don't care if you gamble. Just make sure your family doesn't suffer for it.' And I can honestly say we didn't. In fact, I bought many a new dress with my share of the winnings. To this day, if Ed wins money gambling, the whole family gets a cut. I think he enjoys sharing his winnings as much as he does the actual gambling.

Our family was growing and we had to find a larger place to live. Ed's sister, Anne, and her husband, Joe Stencil, had built a small bungalow up the hill from the family homestead. They wanted to sell since they were interested in moving into a bigger place in Boston. We decided to buy their house and made the move.

Life was good to us. Ed worked at the Daily News and played golf whenever he could. On weekends, he was a starter at Baldoc Hills Country Club. I was busy raising Scoop and taking care of our home. When we discovered I was pregnant again in 1939, we were happy although a bit apprehensive. I started out with morning sickness and couldn't keep any food down at all. Fearing I might lose the baby, Ed had me hospitalized.

The doctor came by and said I could go home as soon as I could keep some food down. They fed me oatmeal, which I detest to this day, but eventually I was able to keep it down and was discharged. On April 14, 1940, I gave birth to our daughter, Janice Lynne, at home. Ed was with me during the birth. He was so nervous and overwrought at seeing me in pain that the midwife present threatened to ask him to leave. Our daughter was finally born, weighing in at nine pounds eight ounces, and Ed was absolutely thrilled.

In 1940, Ed was asked to run for township auditor. Four years later, he ran for treasurer of Elizabeth Township and won the election. That same year on July 7, our third child, Norman Craig, was born at Mcgee Hospital. Our lives were pretty full. I helped Ed with his elected job by typing out tax cards that we would mail to property owners. We also collected money from people who would come to our house to pay their taxes. Come to think of it, we often kept large amounts of money in the house and never thought of locking our doors. How things have changed!

Chess Copeland and his wife, Edith, were good friends of ours. Chess loved golf and both he and Edith were good dancers, so we had a lot in common. One day in 1946, Chess told Ed the Youghiogheny Country Club was putting on a membership drive for new members. There was no initiation fee and the dues were only $20 a month. Things were going pretty well for us economically, so I gave Ed my blessing to join since I knew it was his dream to become a member of the Yough.

On the day Ed came home and said Bill Sullivan had asked him to manage 7 Springs, I was flabbergasted.

"You realize if I take this, it will involve the whole family," he added. Well, I knew Ed had helped Sullivan lay out the course, but I never dreamed he would want us to run it.

"Let's talk to the kids and see what they think about it," I suggested. That night we had a round-table discussion. We really had no idea what we were getting into. A short time after opening the golf course, Sullivan decided to head to Florida and get married. He also wanted to develop land in Florida and asked if we were interested in owning 7 Springs for $240,000!

I had to swallow real hard on that one. But I told Ed, "If you think we can pull this off, I'm with you." Ed, always the gambler, just smiled. "Let's do it," he said.

We had some hard times in those early years, pinching pennies, selling off rental properties and doing other things to make ends meet. All the money we earned would go right back into the business. We enjoyed working together as a family and knew we had to keep the business going since we had quite a few family members depending on 7 Springs for their livelihood. For example, Ed's sister, Emily, and her husband, Frank Korbar, and son Terry worked at the course. My brother, Mooney, was chief mechanic and worked two jobs to make ends meet for his young family. Annie and her daughter, Dolores, also put in long hours helping us get the business off the ground.

Somehow we held the business together and the course kept improving. Golf was becoming recreation for more than just the rich and we were on the ground floor. One of our busiest years occurred in 1959. The steel workers had gone on strike and we offered a reduced rate for anyone collecting unemployment checks! Our customers have always believed in our family for being honest and fair, and they kept showing up, even when they were short of money. We never turned anyone away.

One luxury Ed and I always enjoyed was traveling to Florida for the winter. He hated Pennsylvania's cold weather and we were always looking for something to do as a family. We'd take the kids out of school for a couple of weeks each winter and head for the Sunshine State. Once the kids were big enough to take care of things at home, we would go ourselves and spend a month just relaxing. We would always find an apartment just outside Fort Lauderdale near his brother, Vic.

In 1970, we drove down to Florida. After we were there a couple of weeks, Ed ran across an ad in the newspaper.

"Gen, listen to this," he said excitedly. "A three-bedroom condo for sale, no closing costs, no money down. They want only $20,000 for it. Instead of paying rent each year, maybe we should look into buying a place. What do you say?"

We didn't have any spare cash, but the ad was so promising we went to visit the condominium. It was located on Kimberly Boulevard in North Lauderdale. The condo had three large bedrooms, a living room-dining room combination, a small kitchen and a laundry room. We thought it was perfect.

"How soon can we move in?" Ed wanted to know. Five days later, everything was approved. We had a beautiful but empty apartment and needed five rooms of furniture. Unfortunately, we had no money for the furniture.

Vic had recently gone to work for Tim Kinnucan, heir to the Bayer Aspirin fortune. Kinnucan had hired Vic as his personal secretary, which required him to live in his house. Vic and Elsie moved in with him, putting their furniture in storage. I casually inquired how much money it cost them to store their furniture. When they told me $100 per month, I said, "You can store all your furniture in my new place, and I won't charge you a dime!" They agreed and we had their furniture moved to our place. Everything fit perfectly.

The darkest period in our lives happened in 1976. Ed had developed a pain in his lower abdomen that September. He thought maybe he had pulled a muscle, and went to see a chiropractor, Dan Miller. For a couple of months, Dan treated Ed, but the pain didn't go away. Finally, he suggested Ed see a medical doctor for another opinion. Since we were about to head for Florida, Ed decided to make an appointment once we arrived in Fort Lauderdale.

The doctor thought it was his gall bladder and wanted to do exploratory surgery. Ed agreed to the surgery, but something happened that brought us back to Pennsylvania. It was New Year's Eve. Ed and I were celebrating with friends in Florida, and Janice, Norm and some of their friends were bringing in the New Year back at 7 Springs. Shortly after midnight, I called to wish them Happy New Year. Norm answered the phone and said Jan had been in a snow mobile accident and had broken her pelvis. She would be in the hospital at least two weeks. I told Ed Janice needed us and we should go home immediately.

"You can have the doctor back there take a look at you," I added. Ed agreed and we drove back to Pennsylvania.

Janice was quite a sight at McKeesport Hospital, with her hips suspended in a sling. We visited her and the children, and then made an appointment for Ed with a personal friend and surgeon, Dr. Ripepi. I had to stay home with Janice and the kids. Ed called me with the news that the doctors wanted to transfer him to Mercy Hospital for some tests. He added, "I'll probably be in there for a few days. How about packing some clothes for me?"

Well, I thought if my husband was going to the hospital for a few days, I'm staying with him! It had begun to snow and the weather was turning horrible. Steve and Lois Cindric volunteered to drive me to Pittsburgh. Ed was happy to see the three of us arrive. He was scheduled for a biopsy the following morning. None of us thought anything was drastically wrong with Ed, but we knew the tests were necessary to rule out anything serious. My personal feeling was that he might need a gallbladder operation, if that.

Dr. Ripepi decided against exploratory surgery. Instead, he said he wanted to do a non-invasive procedure to take out a small piece of Ed's liver for a biopsy. We agreed to the procedure.

After the biopsy was completed, the doctor came by. When I saw the look on his face, my stomach did a flip.

"Gen," he said, "I don't know how to tell you this because I think of Eddie as a second father. But there is no hope.

"He has the worst type of cancer of the liver that you can have and it's inoperable. I figure he has six months to live at the most. I have the best oncologist I know on the case, but there really isn't much we can do."

The news was stunning. Unbelievable. Unacceptable. Not Ed, who had been so lucky, so wonderful all his life. Not this. Not now.

I was so grateful for the presence of Steve and Lois. We shed some tears together, while comforting one another. I certainly did not want to face Ed alone when he came out of the recovery room. I didn't know what to tell him. Thank goodness, he was still groggy from the anesthetic, which meant I wouldn't have to answer his questions for the time being. And then I began thinking, 'How can I tell Janice, Norm and Scoop about the death sentence their father has just received?'

Naturally, Janice was devastated when I called her with the news. She had just gotten out of the hospital and was undergoing therapy for her injury, but she insisted on coming to the hospital with me. I called Cathy, Norm's wife, to let her know. She promised to contact Norm, who was in Pebble Beach,

CA., to play in a golf tournament. Then I called Annie and Emily, Ed's sisters. They all made plans to come to the hospital immediately.

Then there was Scoop.

He adored his father. We had just built an apartment for him over the past summer and he was thrilled to be living on his own, independent for the first time in his life. How would he take the news? We had a family conference, and family and friends rallied around me. Offers came from everywhere — let's fly him to Germany for a new experimental drug that hadn't become legal in the United States. Or how about Mexico, where a new drug called Laetrile was being used to treat hopeless cancer patients.

Much of what happened in the next few days is a blur. When Ed was awake and asking questions, we were vague in our answers since we didn't want to alarm him. Norm, Janice and I had decided not to tell Ed what the doctor had said. We just wanted to get him home and keep him as comfortable and pain free as possible. Although we had informed his doctors he was not to be told, one doctor apparently didn't hear of our wishes. While Janice and I were out getting a cup of coffee, a doctor on his team went into Ed's room to discuss his condition and his options.

"Gen, come here," said my husband.

As I hurried into his room, I could hear the young doctor stammering, "I thought he knew."

Ed and I cried together, holding each other tight. Now that the truth was out, it was almost a relief. We talked to the oncologist Dr. Ripepi had recommended, a Dr. Buckman. He said the best treatment available was chemotherapy. He emphasized that chemo would not save his life, but it could extend it by a few months. He also said it was a dreadful treatment to endure and I wondered why go through with it if it couldn't save his life?

That was when a nurse took me aside for a talk. She knew of a controversial treatment by a chiropractor who used holistic medicine. According to the nurse, the chiropractor had had some success with hopeless cases. Willing to grasp at any straw, I told Ed and the family what she had said. They agreed we had nothing to lose by trying it.

Ed's doctors were totally against our decision, but since they couldn't give us any alternative plan other than chemotherapy, we decided to go ahead with it. By the time the hospital released him, Ed had lost about 25 pounds. He was in a lot of pain, but the controversial treatment gave him hope. The chiropractor prescribed massive doses of vitamins, 64 pills three times a day! Some looked the size of a football. The treatment also involved a gallon of lemon juice and water every day. I had to get milk fresh from a cow, nothing pasteurized or homogenized.

We knew of a family that operated a farm near us and they sold fresh cow milk. I remember sitting there, listening to the wind howl while the snow swirled, and thinking of how Ed hated the cold weather, and here he was, fighting for his life in a dreadful winter atmosphere that he disliked so much.

For 11 days, Ed took the treatment. He found it harder and harder to get those vitamins down. Then one morning he started vomiting. Everything came up black.

"Gen, maybe we better try something else," he said weakly. "This sure doesn't seem to be working."

He asked me to call Dr. Buckman and said he was ready to try the chemotherapy.

The doctor was delighted at our choice. He said there were some new chemo drugs on the market that didn't seem to have as serious side effects as the others, and he wanted to try them on Ed. The treatment involved taking the drugs intravenously every three weeks for two years. While Dr. Buckman wasn't very optimistic at the outcome, it was the only hope he could give us.

The treatment didn't go down easy. Ed said it felt like fire going through his veins each time the 30-minute treatment took place. He was given suppositories to prevent nausea. Ed felt queasy back home but he fell asleep quickly and slept most of the night. After the first treatment, he began feeling less pain and started cutting back on the pain medication he was taking. Each time he would go back to the doctor's office, he noticed how the other patients who had started their treatments when he did were no longer there. Dr. Buckman would shake his head and say, "Ed, we can't take credit for this. I think someone bigger than us has a hand in it." I wasn't sure what was happening. All I knew was that my husband was no longer in pain and was beginning to gain weight!

Ed's condition improved on a daily basis. He began getting bored sitting in the house and watching the snow and ice and freezing weather. His oldest brother, Luke, would come by to keep him company and talk about old times with the family or just keep him informed on the local gossip. Luke let it slip to

Ed's friends that he was feeling better and might enjoy a card game. That was all it took. The following day, the doorbell rang. There was his whole gang of friends standing there, holding a deck of cards, and they were all smiling from ear to ear.

Well, Ed's face lit up like a child seeing his first Christmas tree. All that winter, they visited Ed every day, playing cards, chatting and watching my husband come back to life. It was wonderful to watch and I still feel a warm glow when I think of their presence and what it meant to both of us.

Spring came and then summer. Janice and Norm, along with their families, were nearing the time when they would move into their new homes along the golf course. Everything was looking up. Ed was feeling stronger every day. I asked him if he would feel up to having our annual Fourth of July party that had always meant so much to the family. Sure, said Ed, let's do it. We had a lot to celebrate.

And so we did. We invited all of our family and friends, including Steve and Lois. Steve, a former musician who had played with several bands, loved to play the drums and sing. He and his band, The Last Resort, came by and we all had a wonderful time together. Ed looked and felt so good that he asked me to dance around the garage. When the song was over, everybody applauded.

Five years after Ed was diagnosed with incurable, inoperable liver cancer, my husband was pronounced cancer free. He had beaten the Big C. It doesn't come any better than that.

Ed and I are proud of all our family members. Our grandchildren, Dale Kuehner, Mark Kuehner and Lynne Beheler, Janice's children and Norm's children, Craig Rack and Tracy Mocello all are working in the business.

When Janice married Robert Sherman in September 1993, we were happy to add his son, Toby, to our expanding family. Norm married Nancy Traham in December 1993, and her two children, Tina and Todd, became welcome additions to our family. On Nov. 3, 1992, Norm and Nancy became proud grandparents when Tina gave birth to a beautiful daughter, Nicolette Marie Steele. She was our first great-grandchild.

Janice took over the reins at 7 Springs in 1985, after Norm moved to Florida to help Ed with his negotiations to purchase Colony West Country Club. Bob has been at her side since 1987, doing everything he could to make her job easier, from taking greens fees in the pro shop, to being a starter on the tee.

Our son, Norm, jumped right in with the enormous responsibility of running Colony West, which consists of an award-winning 18-hole championship course and an 18-hole executive course. There's also a restaurant and a catering business that can seat 300 people.

Norm met Nancy Trahan after arriving in Florida and after they dated about a year, she decided to come to work at Colony West to help him. They married in Lake Tahoe on Dec. 7, 1993. She takes care of billing in the office. At Norm's urging, her father, Rick Evans, came out of retirement to take some of the workload off Norm. He's 85 and he still works three days a week. Rick and his dear wife, Maggie, have become our closest friends as well as a part of our family.

Dale always figured he would be superintendent at 7 Springs when he decided to go to Penn State after high school to study agronomy. He joined the Florida chapter of the Golf Course Superintendent's Association (GCSA) in 1987, and earned his GCSA certification in 1989, making him the youngest certified superintendent in the organization's history. Dale also became a pioneer in managing turf, using computer technology, and is in demand to give seminars all over the country.

In 1985, Dale began dating Cindy Barron. She was attending college in California, PA. when Dale learned he would be moving to Florida along with Norm and Craig. They continued their long-distance romance until they were married on Feb. 11, 1989. She moved to Florida to finish her education and then began working at the Colony West pro shop helping Craig. When Norm decided he needed her in the office, she took on the responsibilities of payroll and insurance. Dale and Cindy made a dream come true for Ed and me when their beautiful son, Ian Michael Kuehner, was born on Aug. 4, 1999.

Mark was just getting out of the U.S. Navy in 1986 when he decided to join the family business. Dale was living in Florida and that left the job of superintendent of 7 Springs to him. It was a big responsibility, even though he had been working on the course since he was a small boy, but he rose to the task. He joined the local GCSA chapter and began learning the intricacies of managing turf. Anytime he had doubts on how to tackle a problem, he called his brother, Dale, to discuss strategy. Mark was the leader in our area among public golf courses to go to contouring fairways, using lightweight mowers, which, up to that time, only private country clubs had done. It resulted in raising the bar for all the other public courses to follow. We also have the reputation of the fastest, smoothest greens around.

In 1993, Mark met Michelle Navrotski and, after dating a year, asked her to become his wife. The family was delighted when they were married on Nov. 9, 1996. Michelle has worked in Pittsburgh for the Allegheny County Coroner's Office. She is a ballistics expert and is called on as an expert witness to testify at trials all over the country. While we're proud of all their accomplishments, the best one, in our opinion, was the birth of their daughter, Haley Michelle Kuehner, on Oct. 10, 2001.

Craig was 18 when he graduated from high school and set off for Florida to live with his father, Norm, and cousin, Dale, in a condo Ed and I had owned since the early 1970s. Craig had worked at 7 Springs since he was a child, helping his dad and his cousins, Dale and Mark, keep the course in shape. He always thought he would make his life's work at 7 Springs, but fate had a different plan. When we took over Colony West in January 1986, Craig was given the job of running the pro shop. He also helped in the kitchen and even valet parked cars for banquets in the evening. If it needed done, he would do it. From a young uncertain boy who first came to Florida, he has grown into a wonderful man. We're very happy he has met his future bride, Tracy Whalen. They were married on Sept. 27, 2003.

Lynne was our first granddaughter, born six years after her brothers, Dale and Mark. She was too young to work on the course with the boys. Her real love since age two was horses and I remember how she galloped like a horse instead of walking. What a grandchild! She got her own horse, Major, when she turned 12, and never tired of caring for him, even getting up before dawn to feed him and clean his stall. After graduating from high school, she attended Wilson College in Chambersburg, PA. to learn the horse business. Her mother talked her into coming back to 7 Springs to work and to let her love of horses be her hobby. While she was away at school, she met Jim Beheler from Roanoke, VA., and they fell in love. He left his roots behind and moved to Pennsylvania to be with her. While Lynne worked alongside her mother in the pro shop, Jim helped Mark on the course. Lynne and Jim married on July 2, 1994. She still is a horse lover and her riding skills have helped her win trophies in cross country events and dressage.

Tracy is a couple of years younger than Lynne and the baby of the family. When I would have the grandchildren together for a sleepover, she and Lynne always stuck together because of the teasing from Dale, Mark and Craig. Those were wonderful years that I would not trade for anything in the world. Tracy helped out at the golf course during high school. After graduating in 1991, she enrolled at Sawyer Business School in Pittsburgh, where she majored in travel and hospitality management. She graduated with top honors and went to work at the Ramada Hotel in downtown Pittsburgh. That proved to be a very good move. She met Randy Mocello, an employee at the Ramada. Randy wanted to become a Pennsylvania State Trooper and joined the Academy in November 1994, graduating six months later. They were married on May 17, 1997. After their honeymoon, Tracy came to work at 7 Springs. She has been there ever since.

Last but certainly not least to join the business is Toby Sherman, Robert's son, who started out working in the 7 Springs pro shop during the summer months. He worked as a snowboard instructor at Seven Springs Mountain Resort in the winter season. Toby is an accomplished snowboarder and at first thought he would pursue that line for a living. However, Dale and Craig talked him into moving to Florida to help at Colony West in 1998. He went into the pro shop with much enthusiasm and was promoted to manager. In 2001, he moved into his own home. Now he wants to attend school to get his PGA Card so he can teach golf.

We have other family members working at Colony West. Jill DiCristofaro, daughter of my niece, Dolores DiCristofaro, spent several seasons working at the 7 Springs restaurant after graduating from college. During the winter, she would visit her parents in Florida, where they owned a condo on Colony West's number 10 fairway. After dividing her time between Pennsylvania and Florida, she allowed Dale, Craig and Norm to convince her to relocate to Florida, where she now manages the restaurant. She met Steve Pincince, who also works at Colony West, and, lo and behold, they were married on Nov. 8, 2003.

Dolores' husband, John, is a Westinghouse retiree. After he retired, we asked him to work for us at 7 Springs. He does everything from working in the pro shop to helping out in the catering department. When he and Delores visit Florida for the winter, he works as Dale's right hand man on the course. John has been a valuable employee at 7 Springs and Colony West, and we're fortunate he is working for us.

Another valuable member of the family is Terry Korbar, who is our chief mechanic at 7 Springs. Terry and his father, Frank, and his mother, Emily, who is Ed's sister, worked at the course when we first started out. Mark said if we could have two other employees who worked as hard as Terry, we wouldn't need anyone else.

Ed and I have managed to accomplish a lot of things during our lives, but our family is easily our greatest treasure. We have been so blessed to see what we have started and how it has benefited so many members of our growing family. We have two great grandchildren and, with God's blessing, we hope to have more to share our dream."

CHAPTER SIX

In between my running a golf course and playing in golf tournaments, I got involved in politics. I make no apologies for being a lifelong Democrat. My father, as I said earlier, was a coal miner and would most certainly have been involved in the United Mineworkers Union had he lived. I have always supported unions and the working man. In my heart, I know that's the stock I came from and I'm proud to be able to say that.

In 1940, I decided to dabble in politics. I knew something about keeping books and ran for township auditor. I won. Three years later, Bob McClay, the popular Elizabeth Township treasurer and tax collector, died in office. A special election was called and 13 democrats and five republicans filed. I won the democrat nomination and Wayne Peckman won the republication nomination.

When the election was held that fall, I pulled 287 more votes than Peckman out of 6,000 ballots cast. The year was 1944. Call it good luck or what you will, but the township voters seemed to like what I was doing and kept me on the job for the next 18 years. I was still working for the Daily News as a typesetter. The pay from both positions helped my growing family, and I didn't mind putting in the extra hours.

World War II was nearing an end after the bloodiest conflict in world history, and America was getting ready to welcome home our victorious troops. The post-war economy was booming. Jobs were plentiful and our township was growing. New homes were going up all over the place. Elementary schools were under construction in Greenock and Mt. Vernon. All of the high school students in the area were attending McKeesport High and it became obvious another high school was needed.

Dr. Faulk, a strong advocate of higher education, helped organize a committee to find a suitable tract of land for the school. Committee members traveled throughout the area, from Greenock Heights to Rock Run, without luck. Land was expensive and nobody wanted to shift a too heavy burden on the local taxpayers. As township treasurer, I made a suggestion: why not look at a farm the county had up for sale because of delinquent taxes? The farm was in the right location and it could be purchased at a great savings to the township. The house and barn were falling down and the 60 acres of land were covered with weeds and heavy growth.

My suggestion was taken to heart and the board bought the farm at a sale conducted by the county sheriff's department. It was a perfect location for the school. The property was located in the center of Elizabeth Township, Forward Township and the town of Elizabeth. That was how the Elizabeth Forward High School came into being.

For the record, my daughter, Janice, and niece, Dolores Stencil, finished three years at McKeesport High before being transferred to Elizabeth Forward, where they were among the first graduates in 1958. When the old Elizabeth High School was closed, the students were transferred to the new school. Today it is one of the finest high schools in western Pennsylvania, and I'm proud of the small part I played in establishing it.

I had joined the Youghiogheny Country Club in 1946, a membership I would proudly hold for the next 57 years. In 1959, I was elected to the PGA Tri-State and was named treasurer in 1960. After serving as president, I became Tri-State PGA Tournament director in 1968, serving at that post for eight years. One of my most memorable accomplishments was starting a benevolent fund for less fortunate members of the PGA. Under our by-laws, every Pro-Am event or tournament we held would contribute to the fund. Today it operates under another name, but it is still doing the job it was intended to do – help the less fortunate members who have contributed so much to golf.

I'm sure there are some readers out there who are wondering, gee, this guy is so lucky. Didn't anything happen to him that wasn't good? Unfortunately, the answer is a sad yes.

My oldest son, Eddie, whom we later nicknamed "Scoop," was born with a disease doctors call Willys Prader Syndrome. It hindered his development from childhood through adulthood. Eddie would never be quite normal compared with other people his age. Yet he was able to develop into a very special person in our family.

For one thing, he had a great voice and loved to sing. He also had a special personality that endeared him to those around him, family and friends. Scoop could carry a tune very well and all of us enjoyed it when he would break into a song.

I personally supervised the construction of an apartment for him near the 7 Springs club house. There were few things Scoop loved more than being independent and driving the Jeep we provided for him. He worked at the golf course, drew a salary and lived as normal a life as he could until he died of complications from diabetes in 1994. Scoop was a very special person, and we all miss him very much.

Something happened in 1963 that could have had a great impact on the Rack family fortune. The county was purchasing ground for the Round Hill Regional Park, an ambitious project that required a large parcel of land. At the time, the county operated South Park and North Park, with each providing visitors with an 18-hole championship golf course. At that time, the commissioners were elected county-wide. They held a meeting in executive session and decided 7 Springs would be a valuable addition to the Round Hill Regional Park. They even came up with a proposed name – East Park.

The parks director and contractor approached me, and they offered me $850,000 to buy the property, lock, stock and barrel. It was a tempting offer, with a nice built-in profit from what I had paid for the place eight years earlier.

Gen and I discussed the proposal and talked it over with our family members. We turned it down. Today, I can look back at how golf has grown in popularity and I have to conclude that was one of the best decisions we ever made.

RICHARD BOUGHNER, FORMER PRESIDENT OF THE YOUGHIOGHENY COUNTRY CLUB AND FORMER PRESIDENT OF THE WEST PENN GOLF ASSN.:

Although residents of Elizabeth Township for many years, my wife, Jean, and I didn't know Eddie Rack as a person, but only as a name until we finally met Eddie and his lovely wife, Gen. Around here, the name Eddie Rack is something to be respected as a golfer, township official, golf course owner and a living miracle when he defied a diagnosis of imminent death and has lived nearly three decades beyond that diagnosis.

To my way of thinking, Eddie is an excellent example of the home town boy who made good and, while doing so, somehow remained that home town boy.

I have heard his friends say of Eddie Rack, and my wife confirms this: "He is a gentle man and a gentleman.

"I never knew him to be angry with anyone.

"He didn't step on anybody or take advantage of a single person to become the successful man that he is.

"He is a bit of a gambler at heart, so he is willing to take a chance and see it through to ultimate success."

So many times my wife and I have driven along Route 48 past 7 Springs Golf Course and wondered out loud, How did Eddie Rack ever envision out of the hills and woodlands of this area such a successful golf course?

Eddie was club champion at the Yough three times. I know because I lost to him in one of those tournaments.

My wife was impressed with the way he could dance. We would watch him and Gen on the dance floor at the Buena Vista Fire Hall on Saturday nights and just shake our head in admiration. How those two could glide across the floor! Even at his 90th birthday celebration, he danced with his daughter and brought down the house. Made me wonder if maybe the rhythm of the golf swing and the movement of dancing feet might have something in common.

And then there is Genevieve. She is the final component of Eddie's life. His partner, his wife, his lover, mother of his children and the world's greatest grandmother. She can even paint! Gen and Eddie Rack – a truly genuine couple and two people we are so proud to call friends.

CHAPTER SEVEN

Luck has seemed to be on my side all my life, but nothing can compare with the way we happened to get the Colony West Country Club. Donald Trump, eat your heart out!

Gen and I have always loved Florida, with its balmy weather, incredible beaches and year-round sun. We had close ties to the Sunshine State with my brother, Victor and his wife, Elsie, who owned a home there. We also had strong family ties, with aunts, cousins and other relatives who lived in the Daytona area.

My children had taken on a greater responsibility in the day-to-day operations at 7 Springs, giving Gen and I the freedom to travel. If you can find a better place to play golf year round than Florida, tell me and I'll go there. I usually played golf at the public courses when Gen and I visited Florida. I had run into a friend of Steve Cindric's, Walt Axelson, who was an equity member of the beautiful Colony West Country Club. He invited me to play a round with him.

The course had a lovely layout and was lengthy, with holes that challenged a golfer's skills. An award-winning course, Colony West is in Tamarac, just outside Fort Lauderdale. I really enjoyed the 18 holes. When we were through playing, we got into a good game of gin, which was right up my alley.

"We're looking for members," said Walt. "Why don't you join?"

He explained that to become an equity member, I had to put up $6,000. Well, I didn't have the money at the moment and told Walt so, adding, "Maybe I can swing it in a year." That wasn't good enough for Walt. He insisted on putting up the money for me so I could join immediately, and could pay him back when I got the money. I accepted his generous offer and became a member, repaying him several months later.

I soon discovered the club had been floundering. The members had wanted to make it an all men's club, but they weren't getting the membership they desired. They decided in order to attract new members they would have to build a club house. There were 100 members at the time, 50 of them being equity members like myself. All they had then was a small block building that housed a locker room, pro shop and lunch counter.

Members were assessed $2,000 to get the needed funds to finance the proposed club house. They hired an architect, borrowed $2 million and launched the building program in 1982. The club house was completed a year later. It was beautiful, with locker rooms for both men and women, and it had a large swimming pool. There was also an upstairs banquet area that could seat 300 people and a large bar on the upper level. But even that didn't draw the membership they needed.

In the spring of 1984, Lou Pleason, Harvey Howard and Lou Ross came by to see me. They were club members and good friends and they wanted my advice on what should be done to make Colony West successful. They knew I owned 7 Springs and wanted to know if it was feasible to turn Colony West into a public golf course.

I was up front with them: I told them managing a private golf club and running a public golf course were two different things. They pursued the subject and asked if I would be interested in buying the property. They were in a desperate situation and thought it could be a solution to their financial problems.

I promised to discuss it with my family.

As I drove home, I remember being excited over the possibilities. Could we possibly pull this deal off? I couldn't wait to tell Gen about it. Janice's recollections start when I called her and asked if she'd like to own a golf course in Florida. She said, 'You've got to be kidding. What course, where is it and who is going to run it?' She pointed out that Mark was in the Navy, Dale was attending Penn State, Craig was a junior in high school and Tracy was attending grade school. Norm and I have our hands full running 7 Springs. Who is going to run it, Dad?'

I just laughed and said we might have a great opportunity to buy the course that it was a very impressive 18-hole championship course with an 18-hole executive course and they had just constructed a beautiful clubhouse with a swimming pool. Gen was pretty adamant about not using 7 Springs for collateral since we could lose everything we had worked for all those years if we couldn't make a go of Colony West. Once Norm got to Florida, we put our heads together and came up with an offer for the members to consider. We offered each member $10,000, plus we would assume all mortgages and pay all equity members their original investment.

Bob Taylor was president of the club. He had his own group from New Jersey that was interested in bidding for the place. They matched our offer and lobbied the other members and swung support to their side. For a little while, it looked like we were out of the running. Janice recalls how each time she would get a phone call from Florida, things were traumatic. First we would call all excited about the deal and things were looking good. Then it would appear the leaning was going to the other bidders. All of us were on an emotional roller coaster.

In April 1984, things were at a standstill in Florida, so Norm, Dale, Gen and I went back to 7 Springs. The rest of the summer passed without much happening with the Colony West deal, since most of the members left Florida during the summer months to go north. Our family had decided to go for it and do whatever it took to get Colony West. Mark had returned home on leave from the Navy and wanted to work with the family again. However, we all knew that unless we got Colony West, there would be nothing for him to do. That persuaded Gen to agree to put up 7 Springs as collateral for the deal.

Norm went to Florida that winter, determined to

make it work. He and I talked to the members and tried to convince them we would be the best choice as the new owners. What finally swung things our way was when we told the 50 equity members that besides our original offer, we would give them a lifetime membership in the club. They voted to accept our offer.

I was absolutely elated. It looked like we had pulled it off. The elation didn't last very long. They told us we would have to put up $100,000 as good faith money within a week. Well, we didn't have that kind of cash sitting around at 7 Springs. To get a loan from the bank would take longer than a week, I thought. I was convinced the other faction trying to buy the club would be able to get the money and pull the deal out from under us.

Then a good friend of our family, Morley Elton, came to our rescue. We had met Morley through Steve Cindric. He lived in Florida near Colony West and occasionally played golf at the course. I told him about our situation with Colony West. To my amazement, he offered to give me the $100,000 good faith money on a handshake agreement. I couldn't believe it. I told him I would never forget his generosity, that if we succeeded in buying the course, he could have a free lifetime membership. I certainly can never thank him enough for what he did.

Before Gen and I flew back home, I thought, 'If our plane goes down, there would be no record that Morley had given us $100,000.' I hurriedly wrote an IOU on a piece of scrap paper and left it on the table so it would easily be found. I wanted to make sure Morley would get his $100,000.

Janice couldn't believe it when I called and told him Morley was going to give us the $100,000 front money. She thought the worst was over, that we could relax. Wrong. I had assumed 7 Springs would be all the collateral we would need for financing, but our bank in Pittsburgh wanted no part of mortgaging our course for property in Florida, and vice versa, the Florida banks wouldn't consider property in Pittsburgh. We were at another dead end. If we wanted Colony West, we had to find a partner.

Well, Norm loved to fish. Any time he was in Florida, he sought out people to go deep-sea fishing with. One of his friends was a fellow golf pro named Rick Worsham, who was Lew Worsham's son. Rick was the golf pro at Punxatawney Country Club in Pennsylvania and he spent his winter months with his parents in Florida. One day, Rick and Norm were fishing when Norm told him about our problems with Colony West. Norm said we were looking for a partner to put up the cash.

Rick told Norm he had just gotten married and that his wife, Beverly's family owned Fairman's Drilling, a company that drilled for oil all over the world. He said they might be interested in this venture. He promised to discuss it with his wife and get back to him.

Gen and I both knew Rick's parents. Lew Worsham was an outstanding golfer who had won the National Open at Oakmont many years ago. We were also friends with Rick's uncle, Herman Worsham, who was the pro at Youghiogheny Country Club. This was our only hope to own Colony West. Back in Pennsylvania, we traveled to Punxatawney to discuss the deal with the Fairman family. Roy Fairman, Rick's father-in-law, was a true gentleman. We also met Roy's brothers, who were partners in the family drilling business. We told them our family had the know how to run the business, and Rick would be their inside man.

That was quite a year for us, 1985. Gen and I were about to celebrate our 50th wedding anniversary, which we did on Nov. 29, 1985. We held the party at the Yough, with a live band and all our family and friends. I danced with my wife to music from that big band and it was wonderful, especially with the acquisition of Colony West so close. About two weeks after our visit, Roy Fairman called.

"We've decided to take the deal," he said. "Congratulations."

Roy was president of a bank in DuBois, PA. and all the funds for the project went through his bank. There was still a lot to do, many procedures to get through, but the project was rolling ahead to completion.

I called Ed Servov to come to Florida for the closing. On the morning of Jan. 26, 1986, Servov, Gen and I headed for the courthouse to sign the papers to close the deal. Ed suggested we get a bite to eat before we got there since it would probably be a while before we would have another chance. The only place nearby that was open was a McDonald's. I can see Ed eating his Big Mac saying, 'Here we are, on our way to sign a multi-million dollar deal and we're eating hamburgers at McDonald's!' We all laughed at the irony.

The Fairmans were our partners until June 1993. Fairman Drilling was a four-man partnership and one of the partners had died six months earlier. The

81

partnership needed to come up with $5 million to pay inheritance taxes. Another partner was in failing health, so they decided that their interest in Colony West was outside their field of expertise and needed to be liquidated. That meant we had to get financing to buy out Fairman's 50 per cent share. After approaching a number of banks and financial institutions, we were approached by Robert DeAngelis, who steered us to Textron Financial Corp. We pulled off the necessary financing and bought out the Fairmans. While it meant using 7 Springs for collateral, we now had ownership of both courses without any partners. In 1998, we had enough equity in Colony West to refinance and pay off the big mortgage on 7 Springs. Today 7 Springs is free and clear and all of the family members are working hard to keep both courses profitable.

Today Colony West Country Club is rated by Golf Digest Magazine as one of the top 50 public golf courses in America. Norm is manager of the club, and his assistants are Craig and Dale.

MARK KUEHNER'S RECOLLECTIONS:

What I remember most about my grandfather is that the grandchildren were never pressured into feeling we had to stay and work in the family business. I can recall many times when he told us to pursue what we love, and to always remember that no matter what happened in our lives, the golf course would always be there if we decided to come back.

When I became a senior in high school in 1983, I wasn't sure if working at the family

business was something I wanted to do for the rest of my life. It was nice working for my family, but at the time it was just 7 Springs and I knew there was no way the business could support the entire family! At that time, my interest was meteorology, but I couldn't see myself going to college, which I felt was a drag. One day I was talking to another senior at school. He told me he was going into the military and that if I didn't want to go on to college, maybe I should consider that. The following weekend, I went down to the local recruiting office in McKeesport and began talking to representatives of the various branches of the service. I had already decided I wanted to learn more about meteorology. I wasn't crazy about running and long hikes, so I narrowed my choices down to the Air Force or Navy.

The Cold War was still underway – President Reagan hadn't yet knocked down the Berlin Wall – and I knew if I went into the Air Force, there would be a good chance of my being stationed in Europe. No way did I want to spend four years of my life in a foreign country! I decided on the Navy. Now all I had to do was break the news to the rest of the family. When I told them of my decision, they were shocked at first and went through the "Are you sure you really want to do this" stage. After I explained to them that there was really no room for everybody to work at 7 Springs, they supported my decision. In February 1984, I shipped out to the Great Lakes Naval Training Center in Waukegan, Illinois for eight weeks of boot camp, followed by six months of basic meteorology at Chanute Air Force Base in Champaign, Illinois.

A year after I enlisted in the Navy, my grandfather began putting together the deal to acquire Colony West. I remember calling home to hear how everything was going. I'll never forget the emotional roller coaster the family was on as they tried to close the deal on Colony West. One day it was a done deal, and everyone was happy. The next day something would come up and the deal was about to fall through and the family was down in the dumps. This went on for what seemed like a year. My grandmother was against the idea of getting 7 Springs tied up in the deal to buy Colony West. She was concerned that if the country club couldn't make it on its own, we might end up losing both golf courses.

In the summer of 1985, I went home on leave and was at my grandparents' house having breakfast when the subject of Colony West came up. My grandmother wanted to know if I planned on coming back into the family business after my discharge. I told her without expanding the business, there would be no room for me. Unbelievably, that was the straw that made up her mind! She talked to Granddad, and said they needed to do everything possible to expand the business so there would be room for everybody – even if it meant risking everything they had to accomplish the task. I don't know your definition of family love at work, but to me this shows what it is really all about.

We bought Colony West in 1986. In March 1987, I received my honorable discharge from the Navy and went to work at 7 Springs as superintendent. I have never looked back.

RAY GRABOSKI, PGA PROFESSIONAL:

My association with Eddie Rack began in 1948 at Youghiogheny Country Club. I was a caddy and later worked in the pro shop and on the golf course. There were numerous times I caddied for Eddie or someone in his foursome. In those days, Eddie was the number one player at the Yough. He won most of the time and practically made a living from the other golfers he played against. He also took home quite a few trophies for winning those printers' championships.

In 1953, I was drafted and went to Korea as a tanker in the Third Armored Division. After my discharge in 1956, I worked as Eddie's assistant pro. He was great to work for and I had the opportunity of getting my PGA card. Eddie's wife, Gen, also helped out at the shop. I found her to be a neat lady to work with and my respect and admiration for her continues to this day.

In 1958, I qualified for the National Open at Southern Hills in Oklahoma. Eddie and some of the other players at 7 Springs helped me cover my traveling and living expenses. I will always be grateful for their assistance.

I left 7 Springs in 1961 to join Philipsburg Country Club as the head pro. Two years later, I joined Mon Valley Country Club as head pro and worked there until 1997. I seldom saw Eddie until we met in the finals of the PGA Two-Ball Championship, when he and his partner Chuck Scally beat me and my partner, 3 and 2, to win the title.

I retired from my job at Mon Valley Country Club in 1997 and returned to 7 Springs as the teaching pro and advisor. Terry George and I were instrumental in getting Eddie elected to the Golf Hall of Fame, an honor he definitely deserved.

LILA GDOVIC, GEN'S SISTER:

What do I remember about Eddie Rack, my brother-in-law? I remember many special times at his home, those wonderful Fourth of July celebrations, the picnics we had, the flag waving, the music and the feelings, family and friendship.

I remember working on tax cards and typing them out when he was tax collector. I also worked at the family's par 3 golf course for several years. It was my first job after I got married and a good experience because it gave me something to do besides being a housewife.

My son, Larry, worked at the golf course when he attended high school. His Uncle Moon also worked there.

When we think of Eddie Kent, the feelings come out. When he felt alone, he would come to our house to visit because he knew he was welcome and we always enjoyed him. He knew he could be himself because we loved him. We had so many laughs and good times with Eddie and his animals. He always looked up to Larry as an uncle and tried to learn from him. I think it was good for him and Eddie Kent and I know they both felt it.

He told John and me on his last birthday he celebrated that we were his favorite aunt and uncle. We felt he was our favorite nephew, and that is a very special feeling.

ELINOR LAYTON, GEN'S SISTER:

There were five children in our family and we had good parents to guide us. Genevieve is the oldest and married to Ed Rack. I have fond memories of earlier days, with all the families and their children. When Duane and I decided to get married, we thought it would be fun to elope. We asked Gen and Ed to go with us to Cumberland, MD., on April 27, 1937. They said they would. It turned out to be a great day, one to be remembered.

Ed was later elected as treasurer of the township, and Lila and I helped with the tax cards. Later, the family always met at the Racks for the Fourth of July. We always had a good time, and we still get together once in a while. It takes all of us to be happy.

EMILY KORBAR, ED'S SISTER:

My brother, Ed, was 13 years old when I was born, so I don't remember much about him until I got older. One thing I do remember is how he would let me sit on his lap and share his breakfast. By then, he was already caddying and going to school, so I didn't see him much.

My other brothers, Luke and Vic, went to work in the tin mill to support the family. There were five of us. Our father had passed away and there was no help the way there is today. They let Ed go to high school and said you better not forget us – and he never did.

I worked for Ed when he was tax collector and also at 7 Springs. He and his wife, Gen, are a wonderful caring couple. They keep all the family together and are always there if you need them. Ed has helped many people and my son, Terry, has a good job at 7 Springs. Ed has many accomplishments, from being a good golfer, to a successful business owner. But he is still the same loving brother we all know and love. He and Gen have stayed the same wonderful, down to earth people they were long ago. I'm proud to call him my brother.

ANNE STENCIL, ED'S SISTER:

My early recollections of Ed, Luke and Victor was caddying at the Yough and bringing home the money they earned to help our mother. The boys were born in LaSalle, Illinois, and I was born in Milston, Wisconsin.

After my dad died, Mom remarried and Emily was added to our family tree.

I married Joe Stencil and we had a beautiful daughter, Dolores. We were blessed with loving, caring parents, Louis and Mary Volk Rack. I like to think of them as looking down at us with pride.

Toby Sherman's recollections:

If I had to pick one person to model my life after, it would be my Pap!

As a matter of fact, my Pap Rack is the reason I decided to commit myself to working in the golf business. While he personifies the term professional, it would be unfair to label him with just that title. Not only is he a great golf pro, he is a great person. Looking at his life and accomplishments not only in his golf career and business but also with family is what inspires me to be successful.

It would be impossible to mention all the ways in which he has been an influence on my life. I have learned very important business fundamentals from watching him. One of the most important is not to just take good care of customers, but also to try to take care of everyone. He is a great business man without being all business. The kind of generosity he has is very uncommon these days. Ed Rack is the kind of person who would do anything for you. If I turn out to be half the person he is, I will consider that a great accomplishment.

NORM RACK'S RECOLLECTIONS:

Our family opened 7 Springs when I was 11 years old. Before that, we played at the Youghioghieny Country Club in the evenings or on weekends. Dad was the club champion at the Yough and we were all members.

It took Dad and Bill Sullivan two years to build and lay out 7 Springs. Mr. Sullivan provided the cash and Dad had the knowledge of many years of playing golf around the country. In the spring of 1955, Mr. Sullivan called Dad from Florida. He said he had met a girl and was planning to be married in August. He told Dad to open 7 Springs. He promised to make it worth his while. That is how the golf course got started. We sure got lucky when we took over 7 Springs and Dad got lucky again when he beat cancer. It also helps to have influential friends.

I'll never forget the time I caddied for Dad in the U.S. Open at Greensburg Country Club. After 27 holes, Dad was two under par. I studied the scoreboard and told him even if he bogied every hole going in, he would still make the cut! Well, he bogeyed every hole and missed qualifying by a single stroke.

At the age of 12, I broke 90 for the first time, shooting an 84. It was then that I began playing on Saturday mornings with the regulars and became a betting man. We played for 25 cents a hole, and the first time out with Dick and Walt, I lost 50 cents. One said, 'Don't worry about paying,' and my Dad overheard the conversation. He pulled me aside, handed me 50 cents and said, 'Always pay your debts.' That was a good lesson, one I'll never forget.

The summer before my senior year in high school, I was a junior member at the Yough and played in the Club Championship. I was 16 on the first day of the three-day tournament, and turned 17 by the end. I won the tournament. The following year, the club would not let junior members play in the tournament, so I wasn't allowed to defend my title. The following summer, when I turned 18, I also turned pro, working as an apprentice PGA pro for my father at 7 Springs.

After high school graduation, I played on the PGA Caribbean Tour with Jim Feree and Ed Furgol. At the age of 23, I qualified for the PGA tour as a "rabbit.' Having no wins under my belt, I returned home to 7 Springs to hone my skills and work. In 1969, at the age of 25, I qualified for the U.S. Open at Youghioghieny Country Club. It was the first year Arnold Palmer ever had to qualify. He was first low and I was fourth low. Tony Jacklin played in the same qualifier and made it as well. It was an exciting time for my Dad and me. I didn't make the cut, but it was incredible to be called to the tee on Open day. The following year, my Dad approached Frank Kelly and asked him to sponsor me on the PGA Tour. I ended up with a two-year contract. My only success during that time was losing a play-off at the BC Open in 1971. I returned to 7 Springs to work.

From 1972-85, I was a regular in the Tri-State

PGA program, winning many tournaments. I continued to play in invitational tournaments around the country. It was while I was playing at Pebble Beach in 1977 that I was called home on an emergency. Dad was extremely ill, and the whole family pulled and prayed together to see him through this ordeal.

In the early 1980s, my Dad had the opportunity to become an equity member-owner at a golf course near our Florida home. That golf course was Colony West Country Club. He was one of 100 member-owners and, as such, received monthly reports. By 1985, it had become obvious to my Dad that the club was having financial problems so grave that bankruptcy seemed inevitable. Dad gathered the family together and it was decided to make an offer to purchase the country club. My son, Craig, and I agreed to move to Florida, and my nephew, Dale, promised to join us after he graduated from Penn State. With that in mind, we began negotiations. It was good luck that led my Dad to become a member, it was luck that we came up with the offer that swung the deal with the other 99 member-owners and it was my really lucky day because that was how I met my wife, Nancy.

TERRY D. GEORGE, HEAD PROFESSIONAL, LONE PINE GOLF COURSE, WASHINGTON, PA:

"What do I know about Eddie Rack? A very

benevolent family oriented person, epitome of common sense who lives his life and runs his business by the Golden Rule: ' do unto others as you would have done unto you.'

I first met him in 1958 when I was 11 years old. I would hang around 7 Springs to hunt for lost golf balls to sell to the players. Soon, I began caddying there on a regular basis. By the time I was 15, Ed had me working in the pro shop. Everybody who worked for Ed learned how to do every job, cut greens and fairways, change holes, sod, everything. Since I was smaller than most of the others, never more than 110 pounds in high school, Ed worked it so I got the easier jobs.

I remember mowing fairways with a big '7-Gang Mower.' Ed would stand on the horizon with his hands spread out wide, meaning I was to take an extra lap around the fairway to make it wider. He knew wider fairways always would speed up play, and that means more rounds in a day.

Ed showed a lot of trust in me. He and Norm would leave on Sunday afternoons to play in Pro Member tournaments, and wouldn't return until after closing time. Many days, we would have over 300 players. I was only 15, and he still left everything in my hands. I always believed in myself and my ability to manage because Ed believed in me.

During these years, I ate more meals at the Rack's dinner table than at my own. I lived right beside the course, less than 1,500 yards away. But Ed knew if I didn't eat with them, I wouldn't take time to go home. Over time, I became a permanent fixture at their table and felt like a member of the family. Mrs. Rack always referred to me as a third son on their Christmas cards. I always felt that way, too.

Norm and I grew up together. Because he was three years older, he was like a big brother to me. Ed knew my family didn't have much. My father was a steelworker, and there were five kids to raise. So, if Norm got a new pair of golf shoes, Ed always said, 'Get Terry a pair, too.' It was like that with a lot of things.

Ed was Tri-State PGA Tournament Chairman in the late 1950s and early 1960s. I learned a lot about running PGA events since the entries would come to 7 Springs. I learned how to match players up according to ability as well as personalities. That served me well and I became Tournament Chairman for six years in the 1970s. I was named Tri-State PGA Golf Professional of the Year in 1983, due mainly to my work as Tournament Chairman. It was Ed's ideas and training that earned me that honor.

Ed founded the Tri-State Open in 1964. A year later, he was Tournament Chairman and wanted to really promote the tournament. He secured the site at Chartiers Country Club, but he knew he needed a few tour players to draw the crowds. At the time, Arnold Palmer had just won the Masters for the fourth time. Being from Latrobe, Arnie is a member of the Tri-State PGA. Ed checked Arnold's tour schedule and called him up. Somehow, he was able to get the reigning Masters Champion and several other Tour players to attend. We had the biggest galleries ever for that tournament.

When I was a young golf professional, I qualified to play in my first PGA Club Professional Championship. The tournament was to be held in Oakland in the fall. I was just a poor kid from Elizabeth Township, so Ed immediately took a set of irons and woods from the pro shop and set up a raffle. He raised over $1,000 to pay for my airplane ticket, hotel, meals, caddie fees, etc. for that entire week. Of course, he encouraged all the players at 7 Springs to buy a ticket. Once again, Ed's generosity had come through.

When Ed was in his mid-50s and Norm and I were in our twenties, we all qualified in the local tournament for the U.S. Open. The area newspapers interviewed Ed about the fact that three pros from the same public golf course had qualified for the U.S. Open. Ed said if he qualified in the upcoming sectionals for the National and either Norm or I became the first alternate, he would withdraw.

Ed touched a lot of people in so many ways. When the Mon Valley mills were running full tilt in the 1950s through the 1970s, 7 Springs' main business came from the steel workers. Ed made them all feel like they were members at Oakmont. They all appreciated him.

With Ed's guidance, I became a better than average player. But I realized early on that I didn't have the length for the PGA Tour. When I was 21 years old, I told Ed I would like to work in Florida that winter to gain private club experience. Ed called his friend, Lew Worsham, then pro at Oakmont and Coral Ridge in Fort Lauderdale, Florida. On Ed's recommendation, Lew hired me. I spent nine winters working for him. While at Coral Ridge, I made many contacts, one of which led me to my current position. I have been the head pro at Lone Pine Golf Club for 29 years, and I owe it all to Ed Rack.

I don't get back to Elizabeth much any more, but one of the proudest moments of my life came last fall when Ed Rack was inducted into the Tri-State PGA Hall of Fame. I was so proud to have nominated him. In order to be accepted into the Hall of Fame, a candidate must receive 80 per cent of the committee's votes. Ed Rack was the only candidate to receive a unanimous vote. He was so proud that evening, but little did he know I have never been more gratified in my life than to see him inducted.

(Author's Note: In 1983, the Tri-State Section, PGA of America named Terry George Golf Professional of the Year. He played in the 1980 Tri-State PGA Match Play Championship, and qualified for and competed in seven National Club Pro Championships. He has been a Class A-1 member of the PGA since 1970).

TRACY MOCELLO, ASSISTANT MANAGER, 7 SPRINGS, AND EDDIE'S YOUNGEST GRANDCHILD:

96

I'm the youngest of five grandchildren. I was only three years old when we moved onto the golf course. That was also the year he was diagnosed with cancer.

Grand pap would always come up to us and ask what we were doing and what we were up to, even if it didn't pertain to business. He is a very kind and caring person. I loved the way he would walk up and rub my ear between his two fingers. What I remember most about him was if he won, we won. Every time.

I remember getting a call early one morning to go to work. Now to be honest, I am not an early person. My job then was to walk over to the golf course and pick up range balls. I also remember Vie putting me to work in the kitchen. I wasn't tall enough to reach the counter and make coleslaw, so I'd sit on a bar stool. I also helped make hamburger patties and would get hot dogs for our customers.

Uncle Vic, my grand pap's brother, would come up from his home in Florida and spend the summers with us. While he was here, he would work in the pro shop. I would come over to the club to help him and sit on his lap, while we bagged tees and worked the cash register.

Lynne and I would take a golf cart and head out to hole number seven, where we would sell fresh lemonade and golf balls. We also held picnics under the big tree on number five, and walk from our grandparents' house with our Dick Tracy lunch boxes. I can even remember what we ate – gingerbread man cookies, brick cheese, a piece of fruit and apple or white grape juice.

We loved sleeping over at Gram and Pap's house on weekends. I remember Pap watching the baseball games on his TV in the family room. That meant we kids would have to be quiet or go downstairs. He didn't want anybody to disturb him when he was watching the Pirates! The boys would always bother the girls, naturally, so we had to split up – boys downstairs, girls upstairs. We would make tents with Gram's blankets and sheets, and the boys would make tents. Then Lynne and I would cry, so Gram had to find more blankets so Lynne and I could make our own tents upstairs. What fun!

My cousin, Lynne, and I loved dressing up in Gram's old nightgowns and shoes, pretending we were movie stars. We had them in a closet to play with anytime we slept over. I remember my Mom coming to pick us up and rolling her eyes when she saw the mess we had made. But Gram would always say, 'It's okay, I have tomorrow to clean up.' Mom wouldn't let us do that at home. No way.

Easter always meant egg coloring time. Mom and Aunt Janice would drop us kids off at Gram's house and to color eggs. We couldn't share the five bowls for the various dye colors. Of course not. Each of us had to have our own bowls of dye. That was a lot of bowls, but Gram didn't mind. She'd put out plastic and old tablecloths and other stuff on the floor to keep us from making too big of a mess, and we would all get into coloring eggs. When we hunted for the hidden Easter eggs, the boys would always try to dominate the girls. Since the boys were bigger, they found most of the eggs. Gram would always make sure we had two Easter egg hunts – one for the boys and one for the girls. That was her idea of fair play.

What else did we do? Oh, we would go to Gram's to spend the afternoon and help her make pie dough. She would give the extra dough to Lynne and me, and when we were finished, it was as tough as shoe leather. We would make cinnamon strips out of it. Mom and Aunt Janice would pretend to taste our creations. They said it was delicious, but of course, it was awful.

Each Fourth of July, Gram and Pap would host a big holiday picnic. There had to be at least a hundred people there – family, friends, people Pap worked with. And there would always be live music to entertain us and so much food! The picnic would start in the afternoon and last into the night, sometimes all night long, and it was wonderful.

There may be better grandparents or a better family than mine, but I doubt it. I strongly doubt it."

JANICE SHERMAN (EDDIE'S DAUGHTER) SHARES HER RECOLLECTIONS:

When our family first began sitting around the dinner table to discuss the idea of buying 7 Springs, I was about 14 years old. I had no idea how much of our lives would be involved in this important venture. Dad had told us we would all be expected to work and I thought, Wow, what a great adventure this will be! My cousin and best friend, Dolores Stencil, promised to work and that was all I needed to give my okay.

Dad would gather us kids together where we would practice making change for customers. The original clubhouse was on one floor, with a pro shop that consisted of a glass showcase and a cash register with golf balls and tees for sale. The lunch counter was next to the pro shop. That was fortunate since I found myself getting hot dogs for a customer and then having to dash over to the pro shop to ring up a greens fee.

My brothers, Scoop and Norm, along with Cousin Dolores, me, and our dog Taffy practically lived at the golf course when school was out. We mopped the floor after all the customers had left, and slept on cots in the men's room. Dolores and I had to duck beneath the covers many times when a customer would surprise us early in the morning in the men's room. Eventually, we made our sleeping arrangements in the ladies room, even though it was so small, our heads were next to the toilet. Mother and Dad would always leave around 10 p.m. to go home since Dad had to get up early to work at the Daily News. Mother had to do the washing for the family as well as for the club.

One of the many jobs Dolores and I shared was to sell snacks and soft drinks at refreshment stand on holes 5 and 12 on weekends. There were no restroom facilities at those stands and there were times we had to ask the golfers when they got back to the clubhouse to send someone out to get us so we could use the bathroom. It got so bad sometimes that we would even climb a tree on number 12 and wave a white flag, trying to get some attention. Finally, Scoop would show up in the Jeep and drive us to the clubhouse bathroom facilities before returning us to work. We were busy, but happy. The only time I recall throwing a fit was when Dolores and I were 16 and we decided we were doing nothing but work, work, work! We decided to go on strike.

Fortunately, Mom and Dad agreed that we needed a little more fun. He asked his sister, Annie, along with her husband, Joe, to take us on a mini-vacation to Conneaut Lake Park. We had a great time and when we returned to 7 Springs, the strike was over and we were ready to go back to work.

We didn't see a lot of Dad in the summer, except for a few hours after he would leave the Daily News and before he was off to a meeting or to handle the township's tax business. If he was at the club, he was always on a tractor, cutting roughs and doing the many chores it took to improve the golf course. Mom always prepared an evening meal so the family could gather to talk and discuss any problems. Mostly we shared funny stories about our dealings with the golfers. I remember getting so aggravated when we would sit down and someone would come to the counter for service. I was usually the one who had to get up and wait on them; that made me learn to eat in a hurry. Our reward for all that hard work was to get out of school in the winter and drive to Florida to visit relatives and spend some family time together for a couple of weeks.

Once school started, our routine changed. We would no longer sleep at the club and Mom would pick us up after school to take us to the course. If there were no customers to wait on, we had to do our homework – Mom always saw to that. Weather was a vital part of our lives. When it rained, we would have time to ourselves. I remember praying for snow, especially over Thanksgiving or Christmas, since we could stay at home and not have to worry about the club. Regardless of where we were, Mom always would roast a turkey with all the trimmings.

As I look back, I can now see how hard our mother worked to keep a family atmosphere while we were at the club. Dad was busy with the Daily News and collecting taxes for the township. During the summer months, he would go to each small community in the township where he had office hours so the people could pay their taxes in person. He was very popular with the township residents. Often I heard him talking to Mom after an evening of collecting taxes, and telling her how he had put his own money toward helping a friend pay taxes so the township wouldn't have a lien against that person's property. Dad always had a streak of generosity when it came to family and friends, and that has never changed. Mom would always back Dad. I can honestly say I don't remember a serious argument between them. Dad knew if Mom disagreed with him that it was something she felt strongly about and he would usually back down. I know much of Dad's success was because of Mother. She never stood in his way or made him feel guilty or miserable because he wasn't with us all of the time

One of Dad's favorite methods of relaxing was to play cards. There was a big round table in the club house where his friends would gather to play pinochle or gin. They nicknamed him "Lucky" because he would win most of the time. Mom never objected to his playing because she knew it was relaxing and he enjoyed himself with his friends. She always said, "I know he would never mortgage the Lower 40. He's a smart gambler and always knows when to quit." Besides, Mom got many a new dress with her share of his winnings.

People call Dad lucky, but I think his family is really the lucky ones.

Dad married the perfect woman to be his helpmate and mother of his children. He was never afraid to take a chance on any opportunity that came by his way, with Mom's blessings, of course. He has always been a fair and generous man with everybody – family, the golfers who play at 7 Springs and friends. My Dad would never hesitate to give a customer a few pointers about that person's golf game. I remember a number of occasions when people who didn't have enough money for green fees would be permitted to play. Dad remembered how it was when he was a kid with no money, and how much it meant when somebody helped him.

Growing up in a loving family that shares everything, the good times as well as the bad, is one of the luckiest things that can happen to a person. Even today, Mom and Dad are happiest when they are able to give to their family. My husband, Robert, said it this way, 'Somebody made a famous quote, 'The harder I work, the luckier I get.' That sums up my Dad to a T."

LYNNE BEHELER, ASSISTANT MANAGER AT 7 SPRINGS, AND EDDIE'S GRANDDAUGHTER:

My recollections of my grandfather are mostly from stories my mother and brothers told. But there is one special memory of him that directly involves my own love of horses. I got my first horse, Major, when I was 12, and later added Kip, Garth, Mo, Shannon and Bounty. Tracy, my cousin, also got a horse named Rio for Christmas 1983. Major and Rio were boarded at Hoffman's Family farm on Fallen Timber Road from 1983 to 1985. Neither of us was old enough to drive, so we drove everyone crazy with them dragging us to and from the barn seven days a week, 365 days a year.

Finally, grand pap said enough is enough. He decided to build us a barn on the golf course so we could walk there anytime we wanted! Now we didn't have to beat the phone company out of a quarter by making collect calls and not accepting the charges, and nobody had to leave work to pick us up.

Pap contacted Randy Fisher, a contractor friend to build the barn. I read tons of books on proper barn construction and visited every area horse farm for ideas on what I wanted. Randy constructed the barn out of concrete block with concrete floors and made the ceilings 10 feet high with a flat roof. It wasn't exactly what I had in mind, but it was a barn nevertheless. After taking one look at the height of the ceiling, my grandfather asked if we were housing horses or giraffes!

Pap was pretty smart. He had some back-up plans just in case Tracy and I lost interest in caring for the horses. He figured if he added a second floor to the barn, he could turn it into an apartment and rent it out. Eventually Tracy sold Rio, but I kept adding horses. I loved getting up before school, feeding the horses and rushing home to clean the stalls before I could ride. It never bothered me, even after I graduated from high school and went on to college. My grandparents used to call from Florida in the winter and ask how I could care for the horses with a foot of snow on the ground and below freezing temperatures. They understood why I couldn't come to Florida on vacation – I had the horses and dogs to worry about. I could also be the one to watch the clubhouse while the rest of the family was in Florida for business or to improve their tans.

My grandfather always supported my interest in my horses and in my competitions. After my husband, Jim, rebuilt the interior of the original horse barn to house three additional horses in 1994, he decided that wasn't enough. He added four more stalls in a new section in 1997. None of this would have been possible if my grandfather had not wanted to make our lives easier by building the barn in the first place. He also co-signed the mortgage on my house until Jim and I could refinance it in both of our names.

My grandparents are incredible. They have always given us anything and everything, from providing for our careers at 7 Springs and Colony West, to supporting us in our hobbies. I am blessed to have them."

CHAPTER EIGHT

In October 2002, I was named to the Tri-State PGA's Hall of Fame. Richard Bisi, chairman of the Hall of Fame Committee, referred to it as a "Who's Who in golf," with only the most accomplished individuals being able to meet the induction guidelines. They recognized me at a Champions of Golf Dinner at the Churchill Valley Country Club. It was a nice dinner and I had a chance to socialize with a lot of my old friends, while meeting some new people I had never met before.

There are only 23 previous inductees in the Tri-State PGA Hall of Fame. Some of the more prominent names are Arnold Palmer, Lew Worsham, Bobby Cruckshank, Doc Giffin, and Sammy Snead. I'm in pretty good company with that bunch. The TSPGA Hall of Fame was organized to honor professional and amateur golfers at a national, state or regional level of competition who have made significant contributions to the game of golf in the Tri-State area, which, of course, includes Pennsylvania, Ohio and West Virginia.

It's nice to be known for doing something good for a game that has done so much for my family and me over the years.

When I think about what golf has meant to me, it's almost like a dream. It could have easily gone the other way, you know. I could have missed those early opportunities and gone to work in the steel mills as my brothers and so many other young men in this area did back in those days. Don't get me wrong. There isn't anything demeaning about working in a mill. The work is steady, you get a paycheck, you can raise a family and if you're lucky and know how to hold onto your money, you might be able to afford a vacation cabin in the hills or even a boat.

As I sit in my den in my home along 7 Springs Golf Course, I can look through the picture window and see beauty. The golf course, my golf course, spreads out before me with shade trees, sand traps, well kept shrubbery, emerald fairways and greens that are fast, firm and true, thanks to the hard work of my sons, daughter, grandchildren and our hard working employees. It takes a lot of people to make a golf course happen and with good luck and planning, we managed to find those people.

When I was young and growing up in the small town of Turkey Foot, just a short distance from the Youghiogheny Country Club, there were just 15 families living there. And yet, thanks to caddying, that small coal mining community produced three PGA professionals. Walter Duda moved to California and built a par 3 golf course and driving range. I still remember him as a super dresser who gave golf lessons to some of the top stars in Hollywood.

Frank Melegary was the golf professional at Pleasant Valley Country Club for many years. His father served as a greens keeper at the Yough, and his brothers, all seven of them, caddied at the country club. One of his brothers, Durando, worked at the Daily News. We're just one happy family.

I love being in Pennsylvania in July. We always have the big party, the Fourth of July celebration that has meant so much to the family over the years.. Our days here at the golf course are warm and sunny – goof for playing golf and good for living. When the sun goes down, the temperature cools off and the night turns silken and black, with the sounds of katydids, grasshoppers and birds. I spend a lot of my time watching the sun set. Occasionally, lightning will flash across the dark sky. Gen will bring me a cup of fresh coffee and sit down across from me. My loving wife and partner.

In September, we'll head down to Florida to attend a wedding. Craig, our youngest grandson, is getting married. We have a nice house down there and plenty of friends and the golf course is nearby. Colony West Country Club, where I plan to spend a lot of my time, is known for its Sand Trap Lounge. It's a Pittsburgh theme bar, with photos and memorabilia from the Pirates, the Steelers and the Penguins. It was Norm's idea and I supported it. Now and then, one of the professional athletes will drop by for a round of golf or a drink or maybe something to eat. You might see a smiling Mario Lemieux , Joe Greene, Myron Cope, L.C. Greenwood

Lemieux , Joe Greene, Myron Cope, L.C. Greenwood or Manny Sanguillen. We're always glad to see them and treat them like family. And it all happened because of golf.

When Norm came up with his concept of the lounge, he said, "Dad, I wanted to give the place the personality of a Pittsburgh bar." He did that and more. Just ask some of the folks from Pennsylvania who have visited the place and who come back year after year to sip a Budweiser, a Rolling Rock or just to say hello to the Rack family. The Pittsburgh Club – it was Norm's idea – has something like 350 members who meet the second Friday of each month for games, parties and picnics. The address in Florida is 6800 NW 88th Avenue in Tamarac. That phone number is (954) 721 7710 or (954) 741 6111 for anyone who is interested.

I have always remained close to all of my sisters and brothers — Annie Stencil, Emily Icorbar, Vic Rack and Louis Rack, who was my biggest political booster until he passed away 10 years ago.

As I near the end of this book, I realize I haven't written much about my father. To keep the record straight, here goes. Dad was a good accordion player. His brother-in-law, Martin Jontas, played the violin. Together they played for weddings and other social events all over Western Pennsylvania. The Herminie Slovenian Lodge was their main stomping grounds. For a Saturday night wedding, they would receive $25 each. They would begin to play immediately after the wedding ceremony and would play all night through the early morning hours. Both of them wore black suits with vests and deep pockets.

We kids knew when Dad played for a wedding. We would have fun searching through his pockets for dollar bills or change, and, sure enough, we would come up with 30 or 40 bills, along with the loose change. I can still see Dad pulling out his wallet and placing it on the table. Mom, the keeper of the purse strings, would be all smiles with approval as she gathered up the money and put it in a drawer.

My mother was a great cook who made the best roasted stuffed chicken in our neighborhood. She always used lettuce, beets and carrots to complete the meal and to feed her growing family. No wonder why my sister, Annie, became such a great cook. She had a terrific teacher in Mom.

The weddings, of course, were just side jobs to bring in much needed extra money. Dad's main job was coal mining, where he worked hard for little pay. Then one day at work, it happened. The roof made of slate caved in, hitting Dad on his back. His injuries were much more serious than anybody in the family thought. Doctors came by the next day and said he had dropsy. Before they would agree to operate, they wanted $200. We didn't have the money to pay them, so there was no operation. Dad slept for two days and two nights, and then he just stopped breathing. It was 1923, I was 10 years old and it was a very sad day for my family.

I have always been close to my sister and brothers, Annie Stencil, Emily Korbar, Vic Rack and Louis Rack. Louis was my biggest political booster when he passed away 10 years ago. While times change, good family relationships never change. I would like to think that Gen's parents and mine are watching with their approval.